# Every Day with Jesus

# Walking Free

'... [God] has saved us and called us to a holy life
- not because of anything we have done but
because of his own purpose and grace.'
2 Timothy 1:9

## Selwyn Hughes
Revised and updated by Mick Brooks
**FURTHER STUDY: IAN SEWTER**

© CWR 2012. Dated text previously published as *Every Day
with Jesus: The Pacesetters* (Jan/Feb 2002) by CWR. This
edition revised and updated for 2012 by Mick Brooks.

CWR, Waverley Abbey House, Waverley Lane, Farnham, Surrey GU9 8EP, UK
**Tel: 01252 784700** Email: mail@cwr.org.uk
Registered Charity No. 294387. Registered Limited Company No. 1990308.

Unless otherwise stated, all Scripture quotations are from the Holy Bible,
New International Version. © International Bible Society.

Cover image: Getty/Robert D. Barnes
Quiet Time image: sxc.hu/hariparmer
Printed in England by Linney Print

MIX
Paper from
responsible sources
FSC® C015900

*Every Day with Jesus* is available in **large print** from CWR. It is also available on **audio and DAISY**
in the UK and Eire for the sole use of those with a visual impairment worse than N12, or who are
registered blind. For details please contact **Torch Trust for the Blind**, Tel: 01858 438260.
Torch Trust for the Blind, Torch House, Torch Way, Northampton Road, Market Harborough, LE16 9HL.

# A word of introduction ...

**C**onsidering what to write at the beginning of a new year is something I find challenging. January is often a time for a fresh start, for setting goals and working towards them with renewed enthusiasm. And so I hope that what follows will offer some encouragement to you as you look to the year ahead.

Looking into 2013, I'm thankful for the opportunities there are to develop the worldwide ministry God has given to CWR. We are hoping, for example, to expand our training programme in South East Asia, and to translate into Mandarin of some of our key publications, for distribution in China.

When I consider this new opportunity in China, I am reminded of a hero of mine, C.T. Studd, a pioneering missionary (and accomplished cricketer!). In the 1880s, Studd went to China to spread the gospel. Two years after he arrived there he inherited a vast fortune – and promptly gave it away! He donated his money to various Christian charities in order to invest in the kingdom of God. Here was a man who had known celebrity status, financial success, sampled the 'best' the world had to offer, and left it all behind. He walked freely along life's path, secure in the knowledge of God's sustaining grace.

This issue is all about one thing: 'walking free' in the grace God gives us through Jesus. As we look into the new year, let's fix our eyes on Him, the author and finisher of our faith, as we take our next steps.

Sincerely yours, in His name

Mick Brooks, Consulting Editor

---

Free small-group resources to accompany this issue can be found at www.cwr.org.uk/extra. The EDWJ Facebook community is growing! To join the conversation visit www.facebook.com/edwjpage

# Grace abundant

**FOR READING & MEDITATION - ROMANS 5:1-17**

'... how much more will those who receive God's abundant
provision of grace ... reign in life ...' (v.17)

We cannot know what situations and circumstances we will face in the year that lies ahead, but one thing we *can* know is that, whatever happens, there is grace available to sustain and support us. Often we try to live our lives in our own strength, but our reserves of energy, determination and patience soon run out. We can feel as though we're 'running on empty'. Yet we can take hold of God's grace, which is flowing freely towards us, giving us everything we need to live life to the full.

Over the years I have noticed that Christians often fall into two categories: those who appear to be thriving and those who are merely surviving. Maybe you have noticed this yourself – some people just seem to travel faster along the journey of Christian discipleship than others. We may grow old at the same rate, but we do not all seem to grow spiritually at the same rate. Some people, even though they have been on the Christian pathway for 50 years or more, appear to travel at a snail's pace, while others have covered the same distance in five. Why is this? There are many possible answers, but I am sure that one of the major reasons is this: they have appropriated for themselves what our text for today describes as 'God's abundant provision of grace'. They have opened themselves to God's grace and thus they stride along the Christian pathway at speed. They are walking free, unhindered by the world's distractions.

Has there been a slowing down in your spiritual life lately? Do you feel constricted and restrained? Then tell Jesus now that you want to get back in the race again, moving forward with the most ardent believers you know. Decide now to walk free in the coming year.

**FURTHER STUDY**

1 Sam.
17:20-24,32-54

1. How was David walking in grace?

2. What does it mean to reign in life?

**Yes, heavenly Father, I long with all my heart to move forward with the most ardent believers I know. I don't want to just amble along the path of Christian discipleship. I want to move at speed. Please help me to do so. In Jesus' name. Amen.**

# You *were*

**FOR READING & MEDITATION – GALATIANS 5:7-15**

'You were running a good race. Who cut in on you and kept you from obeying the truth?' (v.7)

**C**an you imagine the concern and even frustration Paul felt regarding some of the Galatian believers? 'You were running a good race,' he tells them. 'You *were*!' Paul had to use the past tense when speaking of their progress.

Perhaps you turned aside from the question I asked yesterday: Has there been a slowing down in your spiritual life lately? Gently I ask you to face it again. Can it be said of you that you *were* running a good race but now you have slowed down? Once you pressed forward along the Christian pathway with energy and enthusiasm. You responded to God's grace and it came in like the waves of the sea – one breaker after another. Yet maybe the moment came when God led you to some new task and you felt overwhelmed. You felt you couldn't go that far with Him, that the demands were too great. Maybe you'd forgotten that God's finger never points the way without His hand providing the strength to accomplish the task He has for you. You need to experience again (as yesterday's text put it) that God does not give His grace sparingly but in abundance. Meaning there is much more grace available than you will ever need. Was that when you began to falter – when God challenged you to a new form of service – to give more of your time, money, yourself? You realise that people who started on the Christian pathway long after you are out ahead and are walking free.

**FURTHER STUDY**

1 Cor. 9:24-27;
Heb. 12:1-4

1. How did Paul prepare for the race?

2. How do we prepare for the race?

If this is your situation, what can be done about it? God needs all of you just as much as He ever did. Think back over your life right now to discover when you began to falter. Then ask His forgiveness for your lack of intentionality and decide to start moving again. Pray this prayer with me:

**Father, forgive me if I have held back in my spiritual life. I long to be in the race again, and to press ahead. Help me understand that Your grace is always available – more than enough. In Jesus' name. Amen.**

# In time of need

**FOR READING & MEDITATION - HEBREWS 4:1-16**

'Let us then approach the throne ... so that we may receive mercy and find grace to help us in our time of need.' (v.16)

**B**efore going any further, let's pause to consider what we mean by 'grace'. Often grace is defined as 'God's unmerited favour'. 'Grace,' says one writer, 'is shorthand for God's redeeming love.' Grace as undeserved favour is a concept that is still used in the business world. Companies sometimes say concerning a claim: 'We do not accept liability for this claim, but we will make an *ex gratia* [out of grace] payment.' They acknowledge no liability, but out of goodwill they make a token payment to which the person concerned has no legal right. And agreements sometimes contain a grace period in which one party freely gives another party time to rectify a fault.

One person made this memorable observation: 'Grace always has a stoop in it. Love reaches out on the same level, but grace reaches down to pick us up.' The best definition of grace I have come across, though, is this: 'Grace is the strength God gives us which enables us to live or do as Jesus would do were He in our situation.' Simple, but sublime.

However, we should not think of grace merely as unmerited favour or the loving kindness of God. It is important to recognise also that it is the inner strength He lends to men and women like us who need an energy other than their own to face and deal with the various issues and problems that life brings. You can be sure of this: the people who walk free on the path of Christian discipleship have received more of the strength which God imparts. I don't think I am wrong when I say that nothing can happen in your life today for which divine strength will not be given. Through God's grace we can face anything that comes providing, of course, we are open to receive of it.

**FURTHER STUDY**

John 1:14-18;
Acts 13:42-43

1. What have we received?

2. What were the congregation urged to do?

**Father, these last words really sum up the matter: 'providing we are open to receive of it.' Forgive me that I tend to deal with problems in my own strength rather than in Yours. Help me to be more ready to take from You. In Jesus' name. Amen.**

# 'Undistinguishing regard'

**FOR READING & MEDITATION – JOHN 3:1-18**

'For God so loved the world that he gave his one and only Son, that whoever believes in him ...' (v.16)

**W**henever I speak on the subject of grace from the pulpit I can almost guarantee that someone will come up to me afterwards and say: 'If grace is available to help each of us move along the Christian journey at a steady pace, then why is it that some people seem to possess more of this grace than I do?' Often I will answer that question with another question, such as: 'Why do you think that is so?' The answers that come are usually along this line: 'Because God favours some more than others.' Does God really have favourites? Is He like some men and women we may know who are biased in their affections and prefer one person to another? Surely not.

**FURTHER STUDY**

Acts 17:23-34

1. To whom was the offer of salvation given?

2. What was the response?

The thought that God takes a liking to one but not to another is unfounded. Consider the text before us once more – the verse that has been described as the greatest text in the Bible. What does it say? 'God so loved *special people in His universe*'? No. 'God so loved the *world*.' That means everyone. And why do we know it means everyone? Because 'whoever believes in him shall not perish'. No, a thousand times no, there is no favouritism on God's part when it comes to giving the gift of salvation, and there is no favouritism either when it comes to giving grace to those who stand in need.

Charles Wesley, the hymn writer, referred to grace as 'God's undistinguishing regard'. So be assured of this: if you feel as though you are not receiving the grace you need in your life to leap over all the obstacles on your onward way, it is not because God is not as favourably disposed to you as He is to others. The problem is never God's unwillingness to give, it is always either our unwillingness to receive or our lack of understanding as to *how* to receive.

**O Father, You who come to every heart with grace and love and an eagerness to give, help me throw open the doors of my heart to Your loving invasion. May my eagerness to receive match Your eagerness to give. Amen.**

# CWR Ministry Events

**PLEASE PRAY FOR THE TEAM**

| Date | Event | Place | Presenter(s) |
|------|-------|-------|--------------|
| Jan – Mar | Developing Pastoral Care (Christian Vocation) (six Thursdays) | Waverley Abbey House | Andy Peck, Philip Greenslade and Lynn Penson |
| Jan | Counselling Training Enquirers' Morning | WAH | Counselling Training Team |
| Jan | Insight into Assertiveness | WAH | Chris Ledger |
| 5 Jan | Transformed by the Presence of Jesus | WAH | Liz Babbs |
| 8-31 Jan | Marriage on Track (for the Salvation Army) | WAH | Andrew & Lynn Penson |
| Feb | Bible Text to Engaging Sermon | WAH | Andy Peck |
| –17 Feb | Bible Discovery Weekend | WAH | Philip Greenslade |
| Feb | Insight into Bullying | WAH | Helena Wilkinson |
| 0-21 Feb | Managing Conflict | WAH | Hilary Turner and Liz Moles |
| 3 Feb | Christ Empowered Living | Pilgrim Hall | Mick & Lynette Brooks |

Please also pray for students and tutors on our ongoing **BA in Counselling** Programme at Waverley and Pilgrim Hall and our **Certificate and Diploma of Christian Counselling** and **MA in Integrative Psychotherapy** held at London School of Theology.

For further details and a full list of CWR's courses, phone **+44 (0)1252 784719** or visit the CWR website at **www.cwr.org.uk** Pilgrim Hall: **www.pilgrimhall.com**

# Saved *and* sustained

**FOR READING & MEDITATION – ACTS 20:13-38**

'Now I commit you to God and to the word of his grace,
which can build you up ...' (v.32)

**D**uring my life I have got to know hundreds of people who have walked free and unhindered, and I have noted several characteristics in them that I would like to put before you as we thread our way through these opening days of a new year. Here's the first of these characteristics: *they are people who know there is grace to be had.* That is the crest and crown of it all.

Many Christians go through life relying on their own resources. Though they know in theory that God's strength is available to help them face anything that comes, in practice they do not live in the good of it. Something that has surprised me greatly over the years is the number of Christians who go about as if God's dealings with them ended when they gave their lives to Him. They talk about being saved by grace, but they seem to know nothing about being sustained by grace. Their spiritual talk is only of their conversion. God does not just call us to be saints – His grace is available to *make* us saints.

**FURTHER STUDY**

Num. 13:27-14:11;
14:20-24

1. Contrast Joshua and Caleb with the other Israelites.

2. What made Caleb special?

We need to be conscious that there is a strength that far exceeds our own resources, which means that we do not need to stumble along the path of discipleship unaided. Do you know someone who is younger than you in terms of discipleship yet demonstrates Christian qualities that you seem to struggle to put into effect – qualities such as an ability to forgive, freedom from jealousy, lack of cynicism, or joy when others do better at the things they themselves would like to do and encourage them for it? And perhaps some of these people just a year or two ago were held back by sin! You can be sure of this: they are people who live in constant awareness that God's grace is available to meet their every spiritual need.

**Gracious and loving heavenly Father, never let me get away from the fact that grace is available not only to cancel sin but also to break its power in me and over me. Help me not just to understand it but to stand upon it. In Jesus' name. Amen.**

# 'They keep it in mind'

**FOR READING & MEDITATION - JOHN 10:1-21**

'... I have come that they may have life, and have it to the full.' (v.10)

**Y**esterday I said that throughout my life I have noticed that one of the characteristics of those who walk free is that they know there is grace to be had. They are aware of texts such as the one I referred to on the opening day of our meditations which speaks of 'those who receive God's abundant provision of grace' (Rom. 5:17). You see, you can only really receive grace if you know it is available to help you get through every problem and difficulty.

You may think this is a simple point to make and that we ought now to move on, but I assure you there are many Christians who live as if their commitment to Jesus Christ was a completion rather than a commencement. They seem unaware of the fact that God's concern is not merely to impute righteousness to them (to regard them as sinless) but to impart it also. Conversion is not something rounded off but something just begun. Walking free is being sure that God has more to give than saving grace and, with this thought constantly in view, we are kept from complacency – always conscious that although we have already received much from the God of grace there is still far more to have.

On the wall of an office in New York where major business deals are transacted there hangs a card which reads: 'We talk abundance here.' We can, as Christians, when talking about the grace of God revealed in Jesus, 'talk abundance'. As Charles Wesley so fittingly describes God's grace:

*Its streams the whole creation reach,*
*So plenteous is the store,*
*Enough for all, enough for each,*
*Enough for evermore.*

**FURTHER STUDY**

Acts 2:42-47; Col. 3:1-17

1. How did conversion affect the lives of the Early Christians?

2. How did Paul show conversion should produce continuance?

**O Father, I am so sure that You have more to give me than just saving grace, but I am not so sure that I keep this in mind all the time. Help me, I pray, to always remember that truth. In Jesus' name. Amen.**

# 'The Enough'

**FOR READING & MEDITATION – GENESIS 17:1-8**

'When Abram was ninety-nine years old, the LORD appeared to him and said, "I am God Almighty ..."' (v.1)

**W**e continue meditating on the fact that walking free and unhindered requires us to know, first and foremost, that there is grace to be had. And not only that, but to keep the thought constantly in mind.

I have chosen today's text because the Hebrew name *El Shaddai*, which appears in our text as 'God Almighty', can also be translated 'The Nourisher of His People'. One Bible teacher suggests that the English equivalent of *El Shaddai* is 'The Enough'. However we translate this name, it certainly conveys the fact that God's resources infinitely exceed our requirements. His sufficiency immeasurably surpasses every demand that we may make upon it. There is grace enough for everything – everything!

**FURTHER STUDY**

Luke 5:27-32;
7:36-50;
1 Pet. 2:1-3

1. What did the Pharisees not appreciate?

2. How does God nourish us?

Has it ever occurred to you that only sinners can appreciate grace? One writer has commented that God may be said to love the angels, but He cannot be said to exercise grace towards them. It is sin, he says, that transforms love into grace.

To the follower of Jesus, the message of grace is the most beautiful message it is possible to hear. Small wonder that when D.L. Moody, the American evangelist of the nineteenth century, was meditating on the theme of grace, he was so captivated by the thought that, flinging aside his pen, he dashed out into the street where he accosted the first man he met and demanded, 'Do you know grace?' 'Grace who?' asked the surprised man. In the words of another of Wesley's hymns:

*Plenteous grace with Thee is found,*
*Grace to cover all my sin.*

All!

**Loving Father, I bow my head in gratitude, knowing that the grace of which I have been reading today has covered *all* my sin. My thanks, my love and my appreciation know no bounds. Blessed be Your name for ever. Amen.**

# Sufficient in suffering

**FOR READING & MEDITATION - 2 CORINTHIANS 12:1-10**

'But he said to me, "My grace is sufficient for you, for my power
is made perfect in weakness."' (v.9)

At present we are reflecting on the fact that God provides enough grace to meet our every need. Yesterday we acknowledged that in God there is sufficient grace to cover each and every sin. But not only is there sufficient grace to deal with our sin, there is grace for suffering too. The passage before us today makes that abundantly clear.

Paul talks about having a thorn in the flesh. Some think it was ophthalmia, an inflammation of the eye. Others believe it was recurring malaria, or epilepsy. One commentator believes it to be an evil spirit that was allowed by God to harass the apostle and so keep him humble. Chrysostom, one of the Early Church Fathers, believed the 'messenger of Satan' was 'all the adversaries of the word ... for they did Satan's business'. It is impossible for anyone to be sure exactly what Paul's thorn in the flesh was. One writer has wittily observed, 'Paul had a thorn in the flesh and nobody knows what it was; if we have a thorn in the flesh everybody knows what it is!' What we do know for certain is that Paul's thorn in the flesh was sufficiently distressing for him to plead with God three times for it to be taken away. Yet it remained. And at last came the comforting word, 'My *grace* is sufficient for you, for my power is made perfect in weakness.' I love *The Message* paraphrase: 'My strength comes into its own in your weakness.'

**FURTHER STUDY**

Psa. 55:22;
Acts 16:16-34

1. What should we do with our cares?

2. How was God's grace sufficient for Paul and Silas?

Take this truth to heart: there is grace not only to cover our sin but also to sustain us in times of suffering. Sufficient! Enough! Are you suffering at the moment? Unwell perhaps? Or facing harassment and persecution? God's grace was sufficient for the apostle in his suffering and it will be also for you.

**O Father, how wonderful it is to know that I do not have to struggle on my own. Your grace is there to sustain me in all things. Pour Your grace into every fibre of my being. In Jesus' name I pray. Amen.**

# Enough for ever more

**FOR READING & MEDITATION - 1 CORINTHIANS 15:1-11**

'... I worked harder than all of them - yet not I, but the grace of God that was with me.' (v.10)

**G**race, we have been saying, comes in sufficient quantities from God to cover every sin, and also strengthens us to cope with every kind of suffering. But there's more – there's grace for service too.

Paul, in our reading today, is defending himself against his critics. Referring to the other apostles, he says: 'I worked harder than all of them.' At first this sounds like an arrogant boast. But he immediately qualifies it by saying: '... yet not I, but the grace of God that was with me.' Believe me, you cannot travel far in Christian service without that. So often our labours for Jesus go unnoticed by others, or unappreciated, or unrewarded (in earthly terms, I mean). They may even be apparently unfruitful. Unless we are empowered by the grace of God, it is so easy to lose heart and give up. But there is no need for that situation to arise because He has grace – grace in abundance – to give to those who need it. If you are open to Him, He will give you the patience and courage to press on. Then, when at last you come to the end of life's journey and look back upon a record of faithfulness, like the apostle Paul you will disclaim any entitlement to recognition or praise and say as he did: '... yet not I, but the grace of God that was with me.'

**FURTHER STUDY**

Eph. 3:7-13;
2 Tim. 4:9-18

1. What was Paul's conscious thinking?

2. Who supported Paul?

There are many things we can do without in this world: we can do without wealth, we can do without social standing, we can do without a lengthy education, we can do without a large circle of friends, but we cannot do without grace. And God has enough for everyone. Now the question remains: is the thought that you don't have to muddle through on your own part of your *conscious* thinking? That's how we take our first steps as one who is walking free.

**O Father, may I always keep at the forefront of my mind the truth that I don't have to rely on my own resources to get through my days here on earth. You are the giver of grace. Help me make that a daily *conscious* thought. In Jesus' name. Amen.**

# 'I want nothing except ...'

**FOR READING & MEDITATION - PSALM 42:1-11**

'As the deer pants for streams of water, so my soul pants for you, O God.' (v.1)

**W**e have been saying that the first characteristic of people who are walking free is that they are aware there is grace to be had, and not only are they aware of this but they keep the thought constantly in mind. A second characteristic I have observed is this: *they seek grace enthusiastically*. They want it more than they want anything else.

Have you ever heard the name Fletcher of Madeley? He was a great friend of John Wesley and the man whom Wesley designated as his successor in the leadership of the Methodist people, though as it turned out he died before Wesley. Fletcher once made an important public statement on an issue that was exercising the minds of many people at that time, and by so doing rendered a great service to the government of the day. The then Lord Chancellor dispatched an official to ask Fletcher if there was anything he wanted in return for the service he had done for the country. 'How very kind,' said Fletcher to the official when he delivered his message. 'But I want nothing *except more grace*.' Imagine the official returning to the Lord Chancellor and reporting: 'He doesn't want anything. There is nothing we have that appeals to him. He only wants more grace.'

**FURTHER STUDY**

Psa. 63:1-8; 84:1-12

1. Describe the attitude of the psalmist.

2. Why would he be satisfied with a lowly position?

This is always the characteristic of those whose walk is unhindered – they look at the rewards of earth in the light of heaven. They know that the most valuable thing one can possess on this earth is grace, and they look for it *enthusiastically*. 'Let me have that,' they say, 'and I can handle anything that comes.' So it is not enough to know that grace is there or to keep it constantly in mind; *we are to want it more than we want anything else.*

**O Father, stir up in me a desire to know You even more and to avail myself of the grace that flows from Your heart to mine. I want to live by grace, not by gumption - relying on Your strength. Help me, Father. In Jesus' name. Amen.**

# 'Ask and it will be given'

**FOR READING & MEDITATION - JAMES 4:1-3**

'You do not have, because you do not ask God.' (v.2)

Today we continue exploring the idea that knowing God is a God of grace is not enough; *we are to want the grace He gives and want it enthusiastically*. Those who walk free on the path of life understand their need for grace and desire it passionately.

An apocryphal story is told about a man who died and went to heaven. While he was being given a tour he noticed an odd-looking building with no windows that appeared to be a warehouse. Having asked to see inside, he discovered that the whole building was filled from floor to ceiling with row after row of shelves. On them were thousands and thousands of boxes, each with a name written on it. After searching for the box bearing his own name, he opened it and found a list of all the things God had wanted to give him while he was on earth – things he did not receive because he had never asked for them.

**FURTHER STUDY**

Luke 8:40-48;
Phil. 3:1-16

1. Describe the attitude of the sick woman.

2. What did Paul want ardently?

Our text today tells us: 'You do not have, because you do not ask God.' When Jesus was here on earth He said to His disciples: 'Ask and it will be given to you' (Matt. 7:7). But why should God withhold things from us simply because we do not ask? Surely, because God is loving and good, He can be expected to pour His blessings into our life irrespective of whether or not we ask. Asking is important for this reason: *it tilts our soul in the direction of receiving*. The very action of asking implies humility and a recognition of dependence on Another who alone can give us what we cannot provide for ourselves. Often when people have told me that they do not receive from God in the way others appear to, I have put this question to them: 'Have you asked?' Invariably they answer: 'No.' 'Then,' I reply, 'why are you disappointed?'

**O God, I see I need to be awakened to reality. I have taken too many things for granted. Please forgive me. Help me to ask more often and tilt my soul in the direction of receiving. In Jesus' name I pray. Amen.**

# The Word of God, with love ...

**... from you,** to Christians in need, both at home and overseas, who seek – like you – to live in the light of God's guidance. A gift to the ministry of CWR will help us to send resources that will deepen the faith of many.

Jesus said, '... let your light shine before men, that they may see your good deeds and praise your Father in heaven' (Matt. 5:16).

Help us to show love to those in need around the world and brighten the light of God.

Please fill in the 'Gift to CWR' section on the order form at the back of this publication, completing the Gift Aid declaration if appropriate.

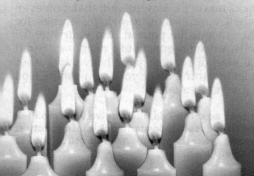

# Asking is not always selfish

**FOR READING & MEDITATION - JEREMIAH 2:1-13**

'They did not ask, "Where is the LORD, who brought us up
out of Egypt ...?"' (v.6)

If, as we saw yesterday, there are many things we do not receive from God because we do not ask, why are we so reluctant to ask? On countless occasions people have told me that during their prayer times they never ask for things from God because, in their words: 'It seems so selfish.' They believe it is impolite to ask God for something for themselves, or feel sure that God will consider them greedy if they ask for too many blessings. Some very sincere Christians regard it as a sign of spiritual immaturity to ever think in terms of asking for things for themselves.

**FURTHER STUDY**

Matt. 6:9-13;
Luke 11:9

1. Which phrases in the Lord's Prayer are to do with self?

2. What should we ask God for?

Of course, if our prayers are *always* geared to our own blessings and we are *always* asking for things for ourselves, most certainly it is a selfish form of praying.

I have always loved the story of the young unmarried woman who constantly prayed in the mid-week church prayer meeting for a husband. 'Lord, give me a husband,' she would say, and then sit down. Her vicar tried to help her towards spiritual maturity by saying: 'It's all right to pray for a husband, but you need to broaden your prayer life. Pray for other people as well as yourself.' So, in the next prayer meeting, she got up and prayed: 'Lord, please give my mother a son-in-law.'

Prayer that is always self-seeking and threaded through with self-interest lacks maturity. Having said that, however, it is not wrong, when appropriate, to ask for things for yourself. Asking for grace to be poured into your life, for example, is not a self-centred request but a deeply spiritual one. It's exactly the kind of request your heavenly Father likes to hear. Don't let anything deter you from asking God for His grace to be given to you. Ask!

**O Father, forgive me that so often I do not receive because I fail to ask. Having learned this lesson, help me to put it into practice, beginning today. Give me grace to see my need of grace, and to ask for it. In Jesus' name. Amen.**

**FOR READING & MEDITATION – 1 JOHN 5:13-21**

'This is the confidence we have in approaching God: that if we ask anything according to his will, he hears us.' (v.14)

A clue as to why we have this basic disinclination to ask was given to me on one occasion when I put this question to a woman in counselling: 'Have you asked God to help you in this?' She replied: 'Asking makes me feel so dependent and helpless.' There's the rub. There is something about our human nature that dislikes and resists helplessness. We just don't like feeling dependent.

Bruce Wilkinson, an American writer, tells how he was faced with the situation of door after door miraculously opening in his ministry yet somehow being unable to shake off the feeling that he was not the man for the job. He sought counsel from a Bible teacher who had been a spiritual father to thousands. 'Son,' the godly man said, 'that feeling you are running from is called dependence. The second you are not feeling dependent you are not walking with the Lord Jesus.' Bruce replied: 'You're saying the feeling that I just can't do it is what I'm *supposed* to be feeling?'

**FURTHER STUDY**

John 15:1-5;
Acts 3:1-16

1. What did Jesus explain?

2. What did Peter explain?

For some this is a challenging truth, but as God's children we are to live in daily dependence upon Him. There are a number of things we can get for ourselves, such as groceries from the supermarket, petrol from a garage, water from a tap, but there is one thing we cannot obtain for ourselves except by asking ... and that is grace. The men and women of the world don't seem to set any great store by dependence, but the sons and daughters of God are to live by it. Though it may make us feel dependent and helpless to have to ask God for things, that's the way He has set it up. To know and accept that, and humbly put ourselves in the way of it by asking, is all part of walking free. So, once again, don't try to struggle through on your own. Ask.

**O Father, deliver me from my dislike of feeling helpless. I see that in terms of my spiritual growth helplessness is what I ought to feel. I am indeed helpless, dear Father. Give me grace in abundant measure. For Jesus' sake. Amen.**

# A prayer always answered

**FOR READING & MEDITATION – 1 CHRONICLES 4:1-10**

'Jabez cried out to the God of Israel, "Oh, that you would bless me and enlarge my territory!"' (v.10)

**A**ccording to some research done by a group of young people in an American church, one of the least read books of the Bible is the first book of Chronicles. That's because the first nine chapters are taken up with the family tree of the Hebrew tribes. This formidable list of names has made even the bravest of students turn back.

Yet, as with all difficult passages of Scripture, there are rewards for pressing through, as Bruce Wilkinson, the writer I mentioned yesterday, discovered. In his well-known book *The Prayer of Jabez*, he highlights the little

**FURTHER STUDY**

Josh. 14:6-15; 15:13-19

1. Describe the attitude of Caleb.

2. How did Caleb's daughter follow her father's example?

known prayer of Jabez, which consists of just 29 words. Before it there are names, and after it there are names, but tucked away in between is this amazingly simple but powerful prayer. There was something about Jabez that caused the historian to pause in recounting his list of names and to give a little more detail about this particular man. You can search the Bible and you will not find Jabez mentioned anywhere else. Yet his prayer has been for many the key to understanding more of God and His grace: 'Oh, that you would bless me and enlarge my territory!' Jabez was not being selfish in that prayer, he was simply asking for what he believed God wanted to give him. God is at work in our lives. Don't be afraid to ask Him for things, especially for His grace. It's there for the asking – and the taking.

Was Jabez's prayer answered? Most definitely. When he asked, God heard his prayer. The following five words are some of the sweetest in the Bible: 'And God granted his request' (v.10). When you ask for *needed* grace be assured of this: your prayer will always be answered.

**O Father, what confidence this gives me as I approach Your throne. Often I am not sure if my request is in line with Your will. Asking for grace, however, is different. Keep me humble, ready and willing to ask. In Jesus' name. Amen.**

# 'Ask, man, ask'

### FOR READING & MEDITATION - PSALM 2:1-12

'Ask of me, and I will make the nations your inheritance, the ends of the earth your possession.' (v.8)

For one more day we reflect on the fact that walking unhindered not only involves knowing that grace is there in abundance but also not being too proud to ask for it. The story is told of a man who was praying out loud and using most eloquent language. His prayer went something like this: 'O Thou who gildest the heavens and settest the stars in place, Thou who hast established the rocks and cliffs around our shores, against whose feet the heaving waters break in ineffectual foam. Thou whose might and power is known throughout the whole universe ...' After several minutes of this one man blurted out, 'That's enough. Ask Him for something. Ask man, ask.' I wonder, are you someone who believes that grace drizzles over the whole of your life at a predetermined rate, no matter what you do? No extra effort on your part is required. Or perhaps you are one of those who believe that because God has been especially kind to you lately He should ignore you for a while and concentrate on someone else, someone more needy than you. This kind of thinking is a trap. Scripture repeatedly gives us examples of people who received things from God because they asked.

**FURTHER STUDY**

Josh. 10:6-14;
2 Cor. 1:3-11

1. Describe Joshua's attitude to life's challenges and to prayer.

2. What was Paul's testimony?

In the psalm before us today God instructs, 'Ask of me, and I will make the nations your inheritance ...' Asking ensures that we do not take God for granted. As I said earlier, it tilts our soul in the direction of God. When we *ask* for grace it shows Him that we are in earnest about receiving it. Already we have made the point that when we ask for grace we do not need to wonder whether or not our prayer is in the will of God. God has made it clear He is willing to give; asking makes it clear we are willing to receive.

**Father, help me grasp this lesson before I move on, for I sense that I am inclined to depend on my own resources rather than on Yours. Help me be more open on this issue. In Jesus' name. Amen.**

# 'Cheap grace'

**FOR READING & MEDITATION - 2 PETER 3:1-18**

'You ought to live holy and godly lives as you look forward to
the day of God ...' (vv.11-12)

**A**nother characteristic I have noticed in those whose
walk is unfettered is this: *they understand that though
grace is free, it is not cheap.* This is tremendously important
because an overemphasis on grace to the exclusion of other
important truths can lead to serious misunderstandings.
As I have said before, truth not held in conjunction with
other equally important truths can quickly become error.

A counsellor friend of mine recalls talking to a young
married man who was involved in an extramarital affair.
When challenged, the young man responded: 'I know I'm
wrong to continue my affair, but you're wrong to
insist I end it. God doesn't want me to continue it I
know, but He'll forgive me. I sense only judgment
from you. God is a God of grace.' I can tell you
this: Christians who hold the view that although
God wants us to obey His commands it doesn't
matter too much if we disregard them will have
to face the many and varied consequences of
their actions. Dietrich Bonhoeffer, the German
pastor who was executed by the Nazis just before
the end of World War II, coined a phrase for this
view of grace – he called it 'cheap grace'. He described it
as 'cheap' because 'it does not consider what it cost God to
make it available to us'. And what did it cost? It cost the
humiliation, death and resurrection of His only Son, the
Lord Jesus Christ.

The more clearly we understand God's holiness and
righteousness, and the more we consider how insistent He
is in His Word that His children live as holy and righteous
people, the more amazing is the concept of grace. 'The idea
of "cheap grace",' says Dr Larry Crabb, 'develops when we
talk about grace before we tremble at God's holiness.'

**FURTHER
STUDY**

Eph. 2:1-10;
1 Pet. 1:13-24

1. Why is
grace free yet
priceless?

2. How should
we now live?

**My Father and my God, if I have never trembled at Your holiness,
then bring me to that point now, I pray. Help me always to keep
in mind that though grace may be free to me, it cost You so very
much. In Jesus' name. Amen.**

# How do you see God?

**FOR READING & MEDITATION – DEUTERONOMY 4:15-31**

'… the LORD your God is a consuming fire, a jealous God.' (v.24)

**W**e concluded yesterday with the statement: 'The idea of "cheap grace",' says Dr Larry Crabb, 'develops when we talk about grace before we tremble at God's holiness.' Are you someone who is in awe of God's holiness before you celebrate and rejoice in His grace? And now, ask yourself the following question: How do I see God? As an indulgent old grandfather who smiles at wrongdoing and says, 'He (or she) will get better as they get older,' or as a God who is awe-ful in His holiness?

C.S. Lewis says that God is 'not … a senile benevolence that drowsily wishes you to be happy in your own way … but the consuming fire Himself'.* The way we view God will be the way we approach Him. If we see Him as indulgent then we will approach Him with the kind of prayer I once came across in the Sunday bulletin of a liberal American church: 'We have done the best under difficult circumstances … we have been badly influenced by our homes and environment … so deal lightly with our lapses, be Your own sweet self with regard to our imperfections, and grant us the power to live harmless lives full of self-respect. Amen.'

Can it be, as Larry Crabb suggests, that our Christian culture has weakened our understanding of the holiness of God by introducing too soon the idea of grace? When I first considered that comment I winced. It seemed a devastating indictment, too painful to consider. But the more I thought about it the more I came to see that it is true. If we talk about grace in a way that makes God an indulgent figure who cares little or nothing about us measuring up to His standards, then we do not fully understand the nature and character of God.

## FURTHER STUDY

Josh. 7:1-26;
2 Cor. 6:14-7:1

1. How did a loving, forgiving God view Achan's sin?

2. What motivates us to live holy lives?

**O God most holy and most righteous, help me not to miss my way on this matter. Give me a fresh vision of Your holiness, Your moral uprightness, for without that vision I may fail to appreciate what grace really means. In Jesus' name. Amen.**

*C.S. Lewis, *The Problem of Pain*, copyright © CS Lewis Pte Ltd, 1940. Used by permission.

**FOR READING & MEDITATION - ROMANS 1:18-32**

'The wrath of God is being revealed from heaven against all the godlessness and wickedness of men ...' (v.18)

Yesterday we raised the question of whether or not our Christian culture has weakened our understanding of the holiness and righteousness of God by introducing too soon the idea of grace. The fact with which we must come to grips (especially those reading these lines who are teachers and leaders) is that we are in serious trouble spiritually if we speak of grace in a way that changes the view of God from One who is the holy and righteous Judge to, in C.S. Lewis's phrase, 'a senile benevolence' – someone who wants us to come up to His standards but is indulgent when we don't.

If my experience is anything to go by, very few Christians today recognise God's incompatibility with sin. The picture many have of God nowadays is of someone who is so kind and considerate that He overlooks our moral indiscretions and encourages us to try harder next time so as not to fail. Instead of starting (as does Billy Graham) with the unpalatable truth – that 'all have sinned and fall short of the glory of God' (Rom. 3:23) – preachers start with news which is easier to digest – that God forgives all sin and is willing to receive us into heaven providing we submit to Jesus, His Son. But the presentation of God's forgiveness must be preceded by the recognition of our *need* for forgiveness. This was how John Wesley preached. 'First,' he said, 'I present the law, then I sprinkle it with grace.'

Notice how Paul writes to the Romans: he presents God not as a loving Father who indulges all the people in His universe and wants them to have a good time. The Almighty, he says, cannot stand sin. The gospel tells the full story of salvation.

**FURTHER STUDY**

Acts 5:1-11;
1 Tim. 1:12-17

1. How does Acts influence your understanding of God's character?

2. How was Paul 'sprinkled with grace'?

**O Father, am I in danger of being brainwashed by a world that has made tolerance a fine art? Am I tolerating sin in my life rather than seeking by Your grace to be rid of it? Help me to renounce all sin, dear Father. In Jesus' name. Amen.**

# Our greatest need

**FOR READING & MEDITATION - ROMANS 3:9-20**

'... for all have sinned and fall short of the glory of God ...' (v.23)

**I** am asking you to reflect with me on the holiness, righteousness and moral perfection of God. It is my conviction that the Church needs nothing greater at this time than a fresh vision of God's holiness. This is what every revival restores to the people of God – it gives them a sense that the God they are dealing with is a holy God. God's standards are perfect. Sometimes in the New Testament the term 'glory' is used to convey God's ideal. In our text for today the word 'glory' is really shorthand for 'righteousness, perfection and holiness'. Unlike us, God operates in absolute perfection. And here's some news that at first sounds bad for the men and women of this world: *He desires the same of us.* Everyone who hopes to relate to God must be righteous because He is righteous.

How different God is from His creation. To relate to me, for example, you don't *have* to be perfect. If you told me your imperfections I would probably respond, 'I am not perfect myself, so I understand.' God is not like that, although He does understand. But He doesn't shrug His shoulders and say, 'That's OK.' There may be times when our goodness is highly commendable. When we take great strides and do good deeds. But are we perfect? Never. By God's standards all human beings fall short.

The law of God was given to make clear to us the state and position we are in. J.B. Phillips translates Romans 3:20 in this way: 'Indeed it is the straight-edge of the Law that shows us how crooked we are.' How true. God is perfect, pure, spotless, and the laws He has made show us how imperfect, impure and full of sin we are. We are pretty undeserving people. Were it not for grace where would we be?

**FURTHER STUDY**

1 Kings 8:46-51; Rom. 3:21-27

1. What did Solomon conclude about human beings?

2. How can we reconcile God's holiness, justice and mercy?

**Father, I see now why grace is defined by some as 'undeserved favour'. What I deserve is eternal punishment. What I have been given is grace. How can I ever thank You enough? Blessed be Your name for ever. Amen.**

# Be Transformed

In her new Lent book, *Transformed by the Presence of Jesus*, Liz Babbs invites readers to adopt a meditative approach and step into the shoes of well-known Bible characters, that we might encounter Jesus in a new way. Here's a taster ...

## SETTING THE SCENE
*(John 4:1-26)*

Jesus was on His way to Galilee and decided to take a shorter route via the village of Sychar. He was tired and thirsty, so He sat for a while at Jacob's Well which was near Mount Gerizim, the site of the Samaritan temple ... Here Jesus met a Samaritan woman and asked her for a drink ...

Talking to a woman and a Samaritan broke many Jewish customs, because the Jews traditionally despised the Samaritans and men did not speak to women during those times. But Jesus not only spoke to the Samaritan woman, He initiated the conversation asking her for a drink of water - thereby crossing all social and religious boundaries to share the gospel with her ...

## IMAGINATIVE MEDITATION

Imagine yourself walking into this story as though you were one of the characters walking onto a film set, but this time you are the person whom Jesus meets at the well.

Take your time to pause in between the questions and sentences below, or use the recording of this meditation voiced over music which is available from my website: **www.lizbabbs.com**

Imagine yourself sitting at the well with Jesus, just enjoying His company ... Is Jesus sitting on your right or your left? What does He look like? What is He wearing? What are you wearing? What is the expression on Jesus' face?

What time of day is it? How are you feeling?

Is there anything you want to say to Jesus?

What is He saying to you?

Now, if you're aware of any worries and anxieties, you might want to talk to Jesus about this and hand your concerns over to Him ... Jesus is our divine burden-bearer and, just as the Samaritan woman left her water jar at the well after encountering Jesus, you might like to do the same ... (long pause)

How does your time with Jesus end?

Now relax and just enjoy resting in God's presence ...

**Transformed by the Presence of Jesus**
By Liz Babbs
ISBN: 978-185345-837-8
**£4.99**

Order using the form at the back or online at **www.cwr.org.uk/store**

# A God most holy

**FOR READING & MEDITATION - PSALM 77:1-20**

'Your ways, O God, are holy. What god is so great as our God?' (v.13)

A recovery of the sense of God's holiness is, I believe, essential for the contemporary Christian Church. If we do not see God as He is then we will never see ourselves as we are. One of the arguments put forward against Christianity is that by talking about a God who expects His children to live up to His standards, church leaders have imposed upon people a sense of guilt and shame, which is an evil and mischievous thing. 'The things we do which the Church calls "sin",' says one writer, 'are very natural and we need not be ashamed of them. We should

**FURTHER STUDY**

Isa. 64:6-7; Luke 13:1-5

1. What did Isaiah explain?

2. What did Jesus explain?

try not to do them, and if we hurt someone else then we must do our best to put things right, but there should never be any sense of shame.'

Jesus, when He came to this world, made it clear that men and women are made in the image of God but that image has been marred by sin. He came to remake that image; that is why He preached repentance and the kingdom of God. Until we see that we are sinners in need of repentance, we are not part of the audience to whom His words were

addressed. Some people may think they are not the ones to whom He was referring, but most assuredly they are. It is impossible to be a Christian without the preliminary consciousness of sin, because without that there can be no real awareness of what it meant for a holy God to save us. The prayer of the hymnist needs to be ours also:

> *O make me understand it,*
> *Help me to take it in,*
> *What it meant to Thee, the Holy One,*
> *To bear away my sin.*

*K.A.M. Kelly (1869-1942)*

**O God my Father, grant that I shall never become so taken up with grace that I forget that though it is free to me, it cost You so much. Help me understand that truth even more fully than I do now. In Jesus' name. Amen.**

# 'A terrible thought'

**FOR READING & MEDITATION - ROMANS 6:1-14**

'What shall we say, then? Shall we go on sinning, so that grace may increase? By no means!' (vv.1-2)

**N**ow we look at another characteristic of people who are able to walk through life free and unfettered: *because they understand what it cost God to offer His grace, they do not abuse it.* One question that is almost always raised when the subject of grace is discussed is this: If God is so full of grace, doesn't this lead to an abuse of it on the part of His people? Won't they say, 'Because God is gracious and willing to forgive our sin we need not worry too much about sinning'? Presenting the truth of grace is challenging, because there are those who would take it to the extreme.

This is the issue with which Paul is dealing in the passage we have read today. J.B. Phillips translates today's text in these words: 'Shall we sin to our heart's content and see how far we can exploit the grace of God? What a terrible thought!' A terrible thought indeed. Max Lucado puts it like this: 'Grace promoting evil? Mercy endorsing sin? What a horrible idea.' For those of you who are interested in Greek, the apostle here uses the strongest language possible to repudiate the idea: *Me genoito*, which means literally 'May it never be.' Anyone who regards grace as a licence to sin has failed to understand what grace is. Max Lucado also says that 'Mercy understood is holiness desired.' Those who have fathomed what it means to be forgiven by a holy God are so overwhelmed by His amazing grace that they want to give themselves to Him in holy and right living.

**FURTHER STUDY**

Rom. 2:1-4;
2 Pet. 1:1-11

1. What was Paul's concern?

2. What was Peter's concern?

There are some who take advantage of grace, but you can be sure that those who abuse it have never been awed by God's holiness and have little comprehension of what it means to be saved by grace. They are likely to stumble along the path of life, snared by every difficulty.

**Gracious and loving God, lead me to a deeper understanding of what it means to be saved by grace, for I see that to really understand grace is to long to live by it. In Jesus' name. Amen.**

# 'A heart set to do good'

FOR READING & MEDITATION - TITUS 2:1-15

'... to purify for himself a people that are his very own, eager to do what is good.' (v.14)

There is a phrase in today's text that touches me deeply every time I read it. It is this: *eager to do what is good.* Because we are the recipients of God's grace, His Holy Spirit fosters within us an eagerness to do good. We don't have to manufacture a desire to do good – the eagerness is already there because of grace. *The Message* puts it like this: 'He offered himself as a sacrifice to free us from a dark, rebellious life into this good, pure life, making us a people he can be proud of, energetic in goodness.' Grace does not spawn a desire to sin, it nurtures a desire to do good. You can be sure of this: the person who is truly aware of grace is a person who will not mock it. As I said yesterday, the person who uses God's mercy and grace as free licence to do whatever they want shows that he or she has not understood grace at all.

**FURTHER STUDY**

1 Tim. 2:8-10;
Titus 3:1-8

1. What is appropriate for those who worship God?

2. To what should we be devoted?

But what if we do sin? What if we are overtaken by it and lapse by doing something that we know God hates? Then, as John tells us: '... if anybody does sin, we have one who speaks to the Father in our defence – Jesus Christ, the Righteous One' (1 John 2:2). Christians will and do sometimes fall into sin, but they do not want to stay there. They will want to get right with God as quickly as they can and have the relationship restored. If they don't then you can be sure there is something seriously wrong with their conscience.

A professing Christian, a family member, once said to me: 'I am about to commit a serious sin, but I know that after I have done so God will be gracious to me and I will be restored.' I responded: 'But will you want to be restored?' He went on to commit the sin, but years later there was no evidence of repentance. I believe his walk with God was hindered – he reaped the consequences of abusing grace.

**O God my Father, help me to demonstrate the eagerness to do good that Your Holy Spirit has implanted within me. Show me how to turn away from the bad and release the good. In Jesus' name. Amen.**

# The scent of danger

**FOR READING & MEDITATION - EPHESIANS 2:1-10**

'... it is by grace you have been saved.' (v.5)

**E**veryone who gives teaching on grace must be aware that the truth can be pushed to extremes. In W.H. Auden's poem 'For the Time Being' the attitude of those who abuse grace is summed up in the following words: 'Every crook will argue: "I like committing crimes. God likes forgiving them. Really the world is admirably arranged."'

The fear that people will take grace to an extreme prevents many ministers from emphasising it. A church leader friend of mine commented, 'If I emphasise grace in the way you are telling me I should then run the risk that people will misunderstand it and be less responsible about the way they live.' Dr Martyn Lloyd-Jones, the great Bible expositor, once declared: 'I would say to all you preachers: if your preaching of the message that salvation is all of grace has not been understood then you had better examine your sermons once again, and you had better make sure you really are preaching the salvation that is offered in the New Testament to the ungodly, to the sinner, to those who are enemies of God. There is this kind of dangerous element about the true presentation of the doctrine of salvation.' Grace has about it the scent of danger. Yes, it can be misused, but it is only misused when it is misunderstood.

When people say to me, 'My problem is that I can't forgive,' I usually respond, 'No, that is not your problem. Your problem is you don't know how much you have been forgiven.' Why do I say that? Because the energy for Christian living comes from focusing on what God has done for us in Christ. Though I have said this before it must be repeated: grace may have come to us freely, but it was obtained at the greatest cost.

**FURTHER STUDY**

Acts 15:1-11;
Titus 2:11-15

1. What was the conclusion of the council of Jerusalem?

2. What was Titus to teach?

**O Father, write this truth on my heart so that I shall never forget it: grace may be free but it was obtained for me at immense cost. May my gratitude be a defence against the entrance of sin. In Jesus' name. Amen.**

# 'The scandal of grace'

**FOR READING & MEDITATION - 1 PETER 3:8-22**

'For Christ died for sins once for all, the righteous for the unrighteous, to bring you to God.' (v.18)

The point cannot be overemphasised: a person who sees grace as free licence to do what they please has missed the meaning of grace entirely. The quotation I included earlier is important enough to repeat: 'Mercy understood is holiness desired.' When I asked someone many years ago how he was able to balance God's desire for us to live holy lives with the fact that grace is available to cover every sin, he replied, 'I treat grace as an undeserved privilege, not as an exclusive right.' This will help you, too, to keep your balance. Live gratefully, not arrogantly.

**FURTHER STUDY**

Isa. 53:1-12;
2 Cor. 5:17-21

1. What did free grace cost Jesus?

2. What transfers have taken place?

One writer, a secularist, wrote about what he called 'the scandal of grace'. This is what he said: 'God wants people to live righteous lives but then He does the strange thing of offering forgiveness in advance. He also says that the more sin increases the more grace increases. It's a scandalous doctrine and doesn't make any sense. Why be good if you know in advance you are going to be forgiven? Why not be like the pagans – eat, drink, and be merry for tomorrow we die?'

Well, grace may seem scandalous to the uninitiated, but to those of us who have tasted of it, it is the most wonderful gift in the universe. Let me spell it out once again: holiness demands that sin needs to be punished. Grace compels that the sinner be loved. How can God do both? Our text for today gives the answer. The perfect record that belongs to Christ has been given to us, and our imperfect record has been given to Him. He suffered, the righteous for the unrighteous, to bring us to God. When first heard and understood this seems too good to be true. But in reality it is too good not to be true!

**O God, forgive me if I am not sufficiently grateful for all You have done for me. Perhaps I do not think enough about Your Son's death for me on the cross. If this is so then please help me to change my thinking. In Jesus' name. Amen.**

# Mercy - the motive

**FOR READING & MEDITATION - ROMANS 12:1-8**

'Therefore, I urge you, brothers, in view of God's mercy,
to offer your bodies as living sacrifices ...' (v.1)

**P**aul's provocative question 'Shall we go on sinning, so that grace may increase?' (Rom. 6:1) has provided a talking-point throughout the ages. Philip Yancey has an excellent response to that question. He pictures a young man saying to his bride: 'I love you very much, but I am sure you will not mind me having a few affairs now and then. You are a forgiving person so just think of the opportunities for enjoyment you will get in forgiving me.' To such a remark, says Yancey, the only reasonable reaction from the bride would be a slap in the face and a 'God forbid!' By his attitude the bridegroom would be demonstrating that he did not understand the first thing about love. Similarly, if our attitude as far as God is concerned is to see how much we can get away with, it proves that we do not have any idea what He has invested in us. Indeed, it is questionable if someone with that frame of mind understands the meaning of the Christian life at all.

In our reading today Paul urges the believers in Rome to offer their bodies as living sacrifices 'in view of God's mercy'. In other words, the incentive for doing good is gratitude for what has been done for us. Those who try to live the Christian life out of a sense of duty are living under law, not grace. This is why Paul begins all of his letters with a reminder of what Jesus has done for us and the riches we have through grace. We should strive for holiness not in order to make God love us but because He already does.

When we truly grasp the wonder of God's grace, the question raised by devious individuals that Paul repeated would never occur to us. As Yancey says, 'We would spend all our days trying to fathom, not exploit, God's grace.'

**FURTHER STUDY**

2 Cor. 5:11-14;
1 Pet. 2:4-12

1. What motivated Paul?

2. How should we respond to God's mercy?

**O God, I see that though it is possible to abuse Your grace, those who truly understand it would never think of doing so. I long to be one who understands it - more and more. Increase my understanding, dear Father. In Jesus' name. Amen.**

# God – the infinite Reality

**FOR READING & MEDITATION – JOHN 1:1-18**

'From the fulness of his grace we have all received one blessing after another.' (v.16)

**A** further characteristic I have observed in those who walk freely down life's path is this: *their knowledge of grace runs to more than theory; they know also how to receive it.* It is one thing to ask God for grace but it is another to open our heart to receive it. As someone has commented, 'It's no good God pouring His grace in abundant measure into our lives if the flow is blocked by an inability to receive.' We have to know how to let grace into our lives, how to take down the barriers. In fact, we must permit it to permeate us so completely that it floods our souls.

**FURTHER STUDY**

Luke 9:51-55; 10:1-11; John 3:19-21

1. What was the experience of Jesus and His disciples?

2. Why might people not receive Jesus?

On my computer I have a file headed 'Quotable Quotes'. While looking for a quote on the subject we are thinking about today – receiving grace – I came across this by E.S. Jones: 'God, the infinite Reality, is pervading us and invading us, and the pathway over which He comes to the centre of our being is the pathway of receptivity.' I would have been tempted to say 'relaxed receptivity', but perhaps for receptivity to be receptivity it must be relaxed. 'You cannot inscribe anything on a tense, anxious mind,' said the same writer, 'for receptivity is the surrendering of all fears, all doubts, all inhibitions, especially the self, for the ego, even in God's presence, asserts itself, wants to be God. It must be surrendered.'

Whenever I have spoken or written on the subject of surrender I have found that people's usual response is to say: 'It's easy to *talk* about surrender, but how do you *do* it?' Let us therefore spend a day or two thinking through this issue because you can be sure of this: people who walk free are those who have surrendered to Jesus and know how to let God be God.

**Father, the idea of surrender does not fit easily with my human nature. I am prone to want to run my life on my own terms, not Yours. But now that my life is Yours I must learn this art. Please help me to do so quickly. In Jesus' name. Amen.**

# Choose CWR
## For Your Conferencing

CWR's two conference venues make ideal venues for your church weekends, Alpha away days, leadership meetings and training events. Both are set in spacious grounds in the midst of beautiful countryside.

### WAVERLEY ABBEY HOUSE

- Day meetings for up to 100 people
- Residential accommodation for up to 44 people
- Eight meeting/conference rooms
- Dining room
- Lounge and coffee bar with pool table
- Patios with outdoor seating
- Views across tranquil lake to woodlands and ruins of ancient Waverley Abbey

**Waverely Abbey House**,
Waverley Lane, Farnham,
Surrey, GU9 8EP, UK
Call our Bookings Team on
01252 784733 or
email waverley@cwr.org.uk
**www.cwr.org.uk/conferencing**

### PILGRIM HALL

- Day meetings for up to 125 people
- Residential accommodation for up to 110 people
- Three lounges and two dining rooms
- Conservatory overlooking the grounds
- Table tennis, pool table and table football
- Heated outdoor swimming pool (May-October)
- Tennis court, putting green and croquet lawn
- Outdoor seating and summer house

**Pilgrim Hall**, Easons Green, Uckfield,
East Sussex TN22 5RE, UK
Call our Bookings Team on
01825 840295 or
email pilgrim@cwr.org.uk
**www.cwr.org.uk/conferencing**

# Taking second place

**FOR READING & MEDITATION - JAMES 4:4-12**
'Submit yourselves, then, to God.' (v.7)

If the expression with which we ended yesterday – 'let God be God' – is new to you, let's explore it further. Our ego was never meant to be central to our personality – despite what modern psychologists say. We were made to have God at the centre of our beings and for the ego to revolve around Him. Thus we are designed not to be ego-centred but God-centred. To let God be God is to surrender our ego into His hands. When we do that, we function as we were designed to. People who have done this are open to receive even more.

**FURTHER STUDY**

Rom. 10:1-4;
Heb. 12:3-11

1. What was the problem of the Israelites?

2. How can we experience real life?

Before going any further I must emphasise that surrender does not mean collapse. Some, I am afraid, see it in that way; they believe surrender involves becoming as nothing and living before God with what someone has described as 'mushy meaninglessness'. Surrender, when properly understood, means that we have a better chance of fulfilling our potential because we are living according to God's design. A truly surrendered person offers to God an alert self, no longer eager for its own way but for *the* way – a self, knowing its place is second, and eager to serve the First.

Once, when talking to a Christian lady about surrender, she asked me, 'If I surrender everything to the Lord does that mean I become pulp?' 'Of course not,' I replied. 'In fact, you become more of a person; you become a person with a controlling purpose – the purpose of following the Person who is above all persons.'

Everybody surrenders to something. One writer puts it like this: 'Everyone goes into the shrine of the heart and bends the knee to something, something that has the place of supreme allegiance.' Can I ask to what you bow the knee?

**Heavenly Father, I lay down the burden of trying to act as God. You are God, not me. So I yield to Your throne. I submit now and for all time. I am no longer centred in myself but in You. Thank You, Father. Amen.**

# The last thing we give up

**FOR READING & MEDITATION - LUKE 14:25-35**

'If anyone comes to me and does not hate ... even his own life
– he cannot be my disciple.' (v.26)

**W**e talked yesterday about the fact that 'everyone goes into the shrine of the heart and bends the knee to something, something that has the place of supreme allegiance'. Can we not see that that is true of us all? Some bow the knee to what others think of them. They don't act, they react. Others bend the knee to themselves. Self-interest is supreme. There are many other things – money, sex, ambition – which may be the centre of devotion. Each one of us must whisper the consent of abdication before grace can flow into our souls in all its fulness. We must say to ourselves: 'I am not the one who is supreme. God is. I bow the knee to Him and to Him alone.'

But didn't we do that at conversion? Yes, we did in measure. But rarely is it done wholly. As we grow in Jesus we see other areas that must be surrendered. The conscious mind is given to Him at conversion but now the subconscious mind – the cause of our divisions and clashes – must be laid at His feet as well. In today's text Jesus says with awful decisiveness, 'If anyone comes to me and does not hate his father and mother ...' Then He makes this statement: 'yes, even his own life – he cannot be my disciple.' Why did He put 'life' last? Because it's the last thing we surrender.

A missionary once told me, 'I gave up my home, family, friends, church, to come to a foreign land. I gave up everything except myself.' To go into the ministry I gave up a career in engineering, but then I found myself preaching the gospel with a great deal of vanity and personal ambition. It is possible to give up lots of things without giving up the self. You see, that is where our *life* is – in the self. It must be surrendered.

**FURTHER STUDY**

Luke 9:57-62;
14:16-24;
John 12:24-26

1. What did Jesus explain?

2. How may acquaintances come before God?

**Father, I come to You to ask for help in this important matter. I struggle to let go of this last thing – the self – but I am willing to be made willing. Help me, dear Father, for surrendering is not easy. In Jesus' name. Amen.**

# Living for Him

**FOR READING & MEDITATION - 2 CORINTHIANS 5:11-21**

'And he died for all, that those who live should no longer live for themselves but for him who died for them ...' (v.15)

**P**erhaps, even after what we said yesterday, you are still finding it difficult to make a full surrender to God. Frequently I have spent time with people who were struggling to surrender completely to Jesus and, as I have watched them, it has seemed as if they were about to say a final farewell to a loved one – the loved one in this case being the self. As I encouraged one young woman to pray a prayer of full surrender she blurted out, 'But if I surrender everything to God then I will be at His mercy.' She thought God was looking for a chance to make her miserable, because she did not understand that His will and her best interests were one and the same.

**FURTHER STUDY**

Deut. 15:12-18;
Luke 9:23-25;
1 Cor. 6:19-20

1. Why might a Hebrew servant surrender his life?

2. In what sense do we already belong to God?

In the first decade of my Christian life I struggled very much with this idea of surrender. For a long while I believed that if I surrendered fully to God He would make me marry a girl whom I found unattractive and send me as a missionary to some remote part of the world. In fact, I had been in the ministry for a few years before I finally said 'Yes' to God on everything. From that moment I have not belonged to myself. I let go of the one thing I owned – myself.

One person I know explains how he maintains a continuous attitude of surrender. 'I begin every day by spending some time sitting in God's presence. After studying His Word, I invite Him to show me if there are any barriers preventing His grace coming through. Mostly nothing is shown me, and by faith I take it that the doors of my soul are open to Him. Sometimes He does show me a hindrance, fear or jealousy. I repent and ask His forgiveness, resolve to put things right, and, after a time of intercession, I go out into the day, serene and secure.'

**Merciful and gracious God, I throw open the doors of my heart today, longing for Your touch and power. Show me if there are any barriers that are hindering the reception of Your grace and I will gladly surrender them. In Jesus' name. Amen.**

### FOR READING & MEDITATION - PHILIPPIANS 3:1-21

'... we who worship by the Spirit of God, who glory in Christ Jesus ...
put no confidence in the flesh ...' (v.3)

**O**ne of the greatest examples of a surrendered life is that of the apostle Paul. What a magnificent model he is for us in this matter of receiving grace. One of the reasons why he was so open to God's grace was because, as he tells us in today's text, he *put no confidence in the flesh*. What was his flesh like? What was it like to be in Paul's skin before he became a Christian? Read once again and try to imagine.

He was 'circumcised on the eighth day, of the people of Israel, of the tribe of Benjamin, a Hebrew of Hebrews; in regard to the law, a Pharisee; as for zeal, persecuting the church; as for legalistic righteousness, faultless' (vv.5-6). 'That's my record,' Paul is saying. 'It may look impressive in the sight of the world but in the eyes of God I was lost and in great need.' Notice how he states that fact: 'But whatever was to my profit I now consider loss for the sake of Christ' (v.7). A few lines further on he says: 'What is more, I consider everything a loss compared to the surpassing greatness of knowing Christ Jesus my Lord, for whose sake I have lost all things. I consider them rubbish, that I may gain Christ and be found in him ...' (vv.8-9). Paul had a great track record but he did not rely on it. He got his priorities straight. When that happened everything fell into place. Once he had no confidence in the flesh he became more open to receiving God's grace.

**FURTHER STUDY**

Luke 22:39-44;
Acts 15:24-26;
1 Cor. 15:30-31

1. Describe Jesus' attitude to life.

2. Describe Paul's attitude to life.

Those who master the inner struggle and put no confidence in the flesh become wonderful recipients of God's grace. They move along the path of Christian discipleship at a rapid rate. Do you know what life is like for people like that? Fantastic! Though problems still arise they are able to handle them with God's help.

**O Father, may the apostle Paul's desire be my desire. I want to walk free, pressing onwards to my high calling in Christ Jesus. This is my desire; help me to reach the goal. In Jesus' name. Amen.**

# Go away and be humble

FOR READING & MEDITATION - 1 PETER 5:1-7

'Humble yourselves, therefore, under God's mighty hand,
that he may lift you up in due time.' (v.6)

For one more day we consider the thought that walking free requires knowledge of grace that runs to more than theory; it also means knowing how to receive it. We have talked a good deal about the need for surrender, but there is one thing more I would like to say about becoming good receivers of God's grace: an attitude of humility is essential.

When I talk about humility, the statement made by the preacher Phillip Brooks always springs into my mind: 'The true way to be humble is not to stoop until you are smaller than yourself but to stand at your real height against some higher nature that will show you what the real smallness of your greatest greatness is.' So stand at your real height, look up at God, reflect on His greatness, holiness and majesty, and consider how infinitely bigger than you He is. Then go away and be for ever humble. A man once told me, 'I used to believe in God but now I don't believe in Him at all. I am coming round to believe that I myself am all-important.' When we lose God we lose our source of humility.

**FURTHER STUDY**

Matt. 11:27-30;
Luke 7:1-10;
John 5:26-30

1. How did Jesus regard Himself?

2. How did the centurion regard Jesus?

After writing that last sentence my telephone rang, and during the conversation that followed a friend asked me which theme I was writing on. When I told him I was exploring what is involved in walking free, and that I was presently writing about humility, he said, 'In the Christian Church I think only the humble can lead, for people who parade their virtues are not fit to lead a procession. We cannot inwardly respond to the proud, however spiritual they may appear to be. Put that into your notes.' So I have, not just because he asked me to but because what he said fits perfectly with our text for today.

**O God, now I have learned that to be a better receiver of grace I need to be a fully surrendered person and one who walks with humility, help me to turn the theory into practice. In Jesus' name. Amen.**

# Graduating in grace

**FOR READING & MEDITATION - COLOSSIANS 2:6-23**
'So then, just as you received Christ Jesus as Lord, continue
to live in him ...' (v.6)

**O**nce again we move on to look at another characteristic of those who walk free: *the realisation that grace has to be used before more is given.* In John 1:16, a text we thought about a few days ago – 'from the fulness of his grace we have all received one blessing after another' – the phrase *one blessing after another* can be translated in several different ways. The New King James Version uses the words 'grace for grace'. J.B. Phillips' translation says: 'there is a grace in our lives because of his grace.' A number of translations use the phrase 'grace upon grace.' When I looked at this verse in a Welsh version I found a word that in English would be best translated as 'succeeding': 'grace succeeding grace.' This, I believe, perfectly captures John's meaning. We must use the grace God gives us in the present to be ready to use the grace which will then succeed it.

**FURTHER STUDY**

Exod. 16:11-21;
2 Cor. 6:1-2;
Heb. 3:7-19

1. What happened to manna that was not collected or used?

2. What is the importance of 'today'?

One preacher I know claims that we *graduate* in the use of grace. 'A man can't walk into a university,' he says, 'and submit himself for a doctorate. He must be a Master first in his field of study. He can't walk in and submit himself for a Master; he must be a Bachelor first. It is only as you absorb learning at one level that you are able to absorb it at a higher level. So it is with grace. We advance. We graduate.' The point he is making is that if we do not avail ourselves of God's grace at one stage then we will not be open to receive supplies at a later stage.

There is an old saying about there being no shortcuts on a straight road. The Christian life is a straight road and we proceed along it one step at a time. We can't miss out any of the intermediate steps. Present grace must be used before future grace is given.

**Father, how patient and loving You are in leading me along the path of Christian discipleship. You love me too much to cut out any step You know to be necessary. Help me to see the wisdom behind Your purposes. In Jesus' name. Amen.**

# Step by step

'Whoever claims to live in him must walk as Jesus did.' (v.6)

**T**he issue with which I am dealing in this section of our meditations is one that I urge you to consider carefully. Many have slowed down on the path of Christian discipleship because, by resisting God's grace at one stage, they prevented themselves from receiving it at a later stage.

Over the years I have talked to many people who told me that they began the Christian life with energy and enthusiasm and moved freely along the path of Christian discipleship. Then they got sidetracked, and it became questionable whether they were moving at all. When counselling such people I have found that there was a time in their lives when God had led them to a new level of surrender, but for some reason they had pulled back. Perhaps it was a new task He wanted them to take up, a challenge about their management of time, a direct appeal to use the talents they had been given, or a word about the need to deal more carefully with their finances. But they had ignored and resisted His voice and followed their own inclinations.

**FURTHER STUDY**

Num. 14:36-45;
Judg. 16:13-21

1. Why were the Israelites beaten by their enemies?

2. What did Samson fail to realise?

I cannot emphasise this too strongly: whenever there has been a slowing down and a slackening off in spiritual things it can often be traced back to some sin of commission or omission. Whenever God gives us a task or a challenge, He also provides the grace which enables us to rise to it. By refusing or running away from the task or the challenge we refuse the grace. And that's when we run on to the sandbank. Refusal to receive grace at that point means we are not offered subsequent supplies of grace. Grace is there, rolling in like the waves of the sea, but we must use the grace first given to be able to use the grace that succeeds it.

**Heavenly Father, how I long to walk the path of discipleship with a tread as firm and steady as that of Jesus when He was here on earth. He never missed a step. Help me to do the same. For Jesus' sake. Amen.**

# Waverley in the Spring

CWR has a Spring Programme packed full of residential courses at Waverley Abbey House, designed to inspire and encourage you throughout 2013 and beyond.

In February we have another popular Bible Discovery Weekend led by Philip Greenslade called **Let's go up to Easter**. Reflect on the Songs of Ascent – Psalms 120-134 – some of the most moving and intense psalms.

As we move into March we will be running our popular Preparation for Marriage weekend, and also our five-day programme **Pastoral Care in the Local Church**. This course gives delegates an insight into how to help others achieve their true potential in Christ within His Church.

The following week is our **Introduction to Biblical Care and Counselling**, another five-day course during which you will learn how God has designed us all to live, why problems develop, and how to begin to help others.

We hope you will join us at Waverley this spring!

**Waverley Spring Programme**
- Let's go up to Easter – 15-17 February 2013
- Preparation for Marriage – 1-3 March
- Pastoral care in the Local Church – Mon-Fri 11-15 March 2013
- Introduction to Biblical Care and Counselling – Mon-Fri 18-22 March 2013

For further information or to book visit **www.cwr.org.uk/training** or call +44 (0)1252 784719.

# Corresponding grace

**FOR READING & MEDITATION - 1 PETER 5:8-14**

'... I have written to you ... encouraging you and testifying that this is the true grace of God. Stand fast in it.' (v.12)

**S**ome Christians I know claim their slowing down on the path of Christian discipleship was due to the fact that God (so they believe) did not provide the grace they needed at a given time. Here is one example.

A man once told me this: 'It is impossible for me to be a Christian in the place where I work. I find myself falling in with the others – using the occasional swear word, telling smutty stories. I try hard to be different, but I end up being one of the lads. What is said about God giving grace in every situation doesn't seem to be true in my case.' As we talked

**FURTHER STUDY**

Num. 15:39-40;
2 Sam. 11:1-27

1. What should David have done on the roof?

2. How did one sin lead to another?

together and discussed his past I discovered that although he attended church regularly and was involved in some of its ministries he was addicted to pornography and had in his pocket at the time pornographic material. 'How did this addiction begin?' I asked. 'It began,' he said, 'when my girlfriend, who was also a Christian, broke up with me. A few hours later I found myself outside an adult bookstore and before I knew it I was inside. For two hours, as I looked at the magazines and videos, all my pain went away. From then on I have found pornography to be a great pain reliever.'

I shared with this man that the very moment he was standing at the entrance to the adult bookstore the grace of God was flowing towards him like a tidal river. The problem was not that God's grace was unavailable; the problem was he did not respond to it. Refusing grace at that point, and failing to repent of his lapse into pornography, made him unable to employ it subsequently. When presented with a dilemma, we always have a choice: to respond in our own strength or to receive God's grace. With every divine command comes corresponding grace.

**O Father, may I never be one of those who claim that lack of grace is the reason for a lapse into sin. With every command there is corresponding grace. Help me never to forget that. In Jesus' name. Amen.**

# Missed grace

**FOR READING & MEDITATION - HEBREWS 12:1-17**

'See to it that no-one misses the grace of God and that no bitter
root grows up to cause trouble ...' (v.15)

**W**hat an interesting instruction we find in today's text:
'See to it that no-one misses the grace of God ...' How
can God's grace be missed? Well, think back to the man
I mentioned yesterday, the one who went into the adult
bookstore. You can be sure that the moment he was being
tempted to go into that place, the grace of God was flowing
towards him. He had a choice – to either respond and receive
of it or to ignore it and turn away. Instead of turning to the
grace which God offered, he turned to the temptation, and
then needed to face the consequences of his actions. That's
what it means to miss the grace of God.

The passage we are looking at says that three
main problems arise when we miss God's grace.
Before considering them let me say that the best
translation of Hebrews 12:15-17, in my opinion, is
that provided for us by J.B. Phillips: 'Be careful
that none of you fails to respond to the grace
which God gives, for if he does there can very
easily spring up in him a bitter spirit which is not
only bad in itself but can also poison the lives of
many others' (v.15).

Imagine hearing that a friend has been saying
some bad things about you. Now remember, at the
very moment the matter is made known to you the grace
of God is flowing towards you to enable you to deal with
it well. But you refuse the grace, and now what happens?
Your spirit becomes bitter, and because bitterness is not a
pleasant feeling you spread it around a little. You fly off the
handle at the slightest thing, and your friends and family
feel the effect. 'What's wrong with him (or her)?' they say.
You know what's wrong. Grace was there to help you deal
with the issue in a Christlike way, but you missed it.

**FURTHER
STUDY**

2 Chron.
15:1-9,16-19;
16:1-14

1. What principle
did Azariah
explain?

2. How did
this apply in
Asa's life?

**Gracious and loving Lord, let me not miss the grace that is so
important to my functioning as a true Christian. Help me to walk
in a manner worthy of the vocation to which I have been called.
For Jesus' sake. Amen.**

# No grace - no strength

FOR READING & MEDITATION - HEBREWS 12:14-29

'See that no-one is sexually immoral, or is godless like Esau, who for a ... meal sold his inheritance rights ...' (v.16)

**W**e spend another day focusing on Hebrews 12:15-17. One possible result of missing or refusing the grace of God (as we saw yesterday) is the development of a bitter spirit. Another one, according to our text, is the possibility of falling into impurity. We need grace to live pure lives, and when that grace is missed or refused we become extremely vulnerable to temptation, especially impure thoughts or deeds.

This is what happened to the man to whom I referred earlier. He found sex to be an effective pain-killer and his mind became, in words used by Dr W.E. Sangster, a 'merry-go-round of lustful images and impure thoughts'. Most of us experience powerful feelings, especially with regard to sex. However, God has provided us, through His grace, with the strength to manage these motivations and desires. If we miss the grace we will also miss the moral strengthening that comes with it.

**FURTHER STUDY**

Gen. 25:23-34;
Mal. 1:2-3;
Heb. 11:24-27

1. Contrast Esau and Moses.

2. Why did God hate Esau?

The third possible consequence of missing or refusing the grace which God gives is that we can lose our reverence for the things of God. Esau did this, says the writer to the Hebrews; he was more concerned with the present than the future. One of the effects of God's grace is that it enables us to measure the things of time against the things of eternity. Self-gratification becomes secondary and is superseded by a desire to discover the purposes of God and bring Him glory. Esau failed by valuing food for his stomach more highly than his birthright (see Gen. 25:29-34). So let this solemn word sink deep into your heart: 'Be careful that none of you fails to respond to the grace which God gives, for if he does ...' (v.15, Phillips).

O Father, help me never to miss Your grace or to refuse it. Gladly I open my being to it, for I see that I cannot depend on my own resources. Strengthen me, I pray, through Your grace. In Jesus' name. Amen.

# When you stumble and fall

### FOR READING & MEDITATION - REVELATION 2:1-7

'Remember the height from which you have fallen! Repent and do the things you did at first.' (v.5)

The point we have been making is that we must be open to receive the grace offered to us in the present in order to receive even more of the grace that succeeds it. The Christian life is a step-by-step progression, and we cannot cut out any step. If we think God overlooks our disregard of His standards and says, 'You missed a step back there but it's all right, carry on and make sure you don't miss one again,' then we are greatly mistaken. Let's look together at one of the many biblical examples which supports this.

Take the case of the Ephesian church, which we have read about today. In one sense the Ephesian Christians were wonderful people, and were commended by Jesus for their good deeds, hard work and perseverance (v.2). Yet they had missed a step in their Christian walk – they had forsaken their first love. How does the Saviour deal with this problem? Does He say, 'I have drawn your attention to this so that you don't fall into this situation again. Now regain your first love and I will say no more about it'? Christ is too good a counsellor to deal with the issue in that way. In verse 5 He highlights three things they need to do.

**FURTHER STUDY**

Psa. 51:1-19;
1 John 1:5-9

1. How did David respond when convicted of his sin?

2. What is our assurance?

One is to *remember* the height from which they had fallen. 'Think about the way things were,' He is telling them. Remembering this would help their spiritual perspective. His second word is *repent*. This is the only way to deal with a missed step. There must be genuine repentance, a turning back to God in humble recognition that one has missed the way. It is not a matter of kissing and making up. There must be heartfelt contrition. Then *return*: 'do the things you did at first.' Notice that returning is the last step, not the first.

**O God, I see that I cannot regain a lost love without remembering, repenting and returning. May the formula You gave to the Ephesian church be the one that I use day by day. In Jesus' name I pray. Amen.**

# Making our 'me' gracious

**FOR READING & MEDITATION - COLOSSIANS 1:1-6**

'... this gospel is bearing fruit and growing ... since the day you heard it and understood God's grace ...' (v.6)

**A** further characteristic of those who walk free, which we will now consider, is: *they know not only how to receive grace but also how to pass it on to others.*

There is a charming, though probably apocryphal, story which has come down to us relating to the childhood of England's present queen, Elizabeth II. It tells how, as a small girl, she was puzzled about the words her father, King George VI, used during the singing of the national anthem, since it began 'God save our gracious King.' As he himself was the king, she wondered if he sang to himself 'God save the gracious *me*.' One thing is certain: if we do not allow God to make our 'me' gracious then the purpose of His grace is thwarted. He pours His grace into us that we might pour it out to others.

**FURTHER STUDY**

Luke 16:19-25;
Rom. 12:9-21

1. What problem of human nature did Jesus highlight?

2. How can we demonstrate grace?

It is here that many of us, myself included, have to put up our hands and confess that while we may be good receivers of grace, we are not always good dispensers of it. During a talk show on TV in which a group of people were discussing the amazing grace of God, one sceptic asked, 'If grace is so amazing why don't Christians show more of it?' There is enough truth behind that question to sting. Charles Swindoll says, 'Grace is not something simply to be claimed; it is meant to be demonstrated. It is to be shared, used as a basis for friendships and drawn upon for sustained relationships.'

So often grace is stifled in relationships. We can be going along fine until someone upsets us, and then showing grace to that person is something we fail to do. The message in the passage before us today raises issues that we might prefer to avoid, but not to confront them is to miss one of God's steps.

**O Father, help me rise to this challenge of being a channel of Your grace. I have no difficulty in relating to You; the difficulty comes in relating to others. Help me be a more gracious person. In Jesus' name. Amen.**

# Not sufficiently Christlike

'... make my joy complete by being like-minded, having the same
love, being one in spirit and purpose.' (v.2)

'If grace is so amazing why don't Christians show more of
it?' That is the issue with which we must come to grips
over the next few days. Many of us feel we have 'arrived'
when, by faith, we are accepted into the family of God. But
a Christian, far from having arrived, is always on the road
as a *follower* of Christ.

There is a prayer, I understand, that has become well
known in Washington. It was offered at an informal White
House prayer group by a Jewish man named Arthur Burns,
at that time chairman of the United States Federal Reserve
System and a man of some distinction. Though not
a Christian he seemed to find pleasure in being
present at the prayer meetings. Naturally the
Christians there treated him with respect even
though they found it difficult to involve him in the
proceedings. For example, different people would
be asked to close in prayer but Arthur Burns
would always be passed by. However, one day the
group was led by a newcomer who did not know
the situation. At the end of the session he turned
to Arthur Burns and asked him to close in prayer.
For a moment he hesitated, and then he prayed
this prayer, 'Lord, I pray that You would bring Jews
to know Jesus Christ. I pray that You would bring
Muslims to know Jesus Christ. Finally, Lord, I pray that You
would bring Christians to know Jesus Christ. Amen.'

**FURTHER
STUDY**

Acts 9:36-41;
11:19-30

1. How was
Dorcas
regarded?

2. What
evidence of
Christianity
was there in
Antioch?

His refreshing directness quite startled those present, but
they took the point: those who already know Jesus need to
know Him better if they are to reflect His amazing grace to
the world around. Rarely are Christians indicted for being
too much like Jesus; far more commonly they are charged
with not being sufficiently Christlike.

**O Father, forgive me that there are areas of my life which do
not reflect the grace which so wonderfully and beautifully flowed
out of Your Son towards others. He was gracious to all. May the
same be said of me. Amen.**

# The blight of disunity

**FOR READING & MEDITATION - JOHN 17:1-26**

'May they also be in us so that the world may believe
that you have sent me.' (v.21)

**T**ogether we must face the reality that we Christians, sadly do not often reflect or relay to others the grace we have been given in the way we ought. Critics of Christianity rarely criticise Christ; their criticisms are reserved for the followers of Christ who so poorly represent Him. Friedrich Nietzsche said, 'In truth there was only *one* Christian and He died on a cross.' George Bernard Shaw quipped, 'Christianity might be a good thing if anyone tried it.'

Take the matter of unity, for example, for which Christ prayed in the passage before us today. Clearly unity is important to Jesus Christ. Francis Schaeffer said that God has given the world the right to judge whether or not Christianity is true by the way Christians live in unity with one another. Our heavenly Father does not want His children to squabble. Disunity disturbs Him greatly. And why? Because 'By this all men will know that you are my disciples, if you love one another' (John 13:35). We so often fail to realise what Jesus meant when He said those words. Read this next sentence carefully: the unity of believers will encourage men and women to believe that Jesus is who He said He was. That means not just agreeing with one another, or resolving all our differences, but loving one another, showing grace to one another. Disunity fosters unbelief. 'Who wants to get on board a ship of bickering sailors?' asks Max Lucado. And Paul Billhemir writes, 'The sin of disunity has caused more souls to be lost than all other sins combined.'

Throughout time writers and church leaders have called the Church to unity, but we still have a long way to go. Could it be that disunity is the reason why we are not winning the world to Christ?

**FURTHER STUDY**

John 13:34-35;
Col. 2:1-7

1. How can we apply the New Testament's new commandment?

2. What was Paul's purpose?

**O God, the thought that the disunity of Your Church may be hindering many from coming to know You fills me with deep sadness. I ask Your forgiveness for any part I may have played in this. Use me to develop unity, not destroy. it. Amen.**

# The choice is yours

'Make every effort to keep the unity of the Spirit through
the bond of peace.' (v.3)

**F**or another day we linger on the subject of disunity among the people of God – a matter that is of great importance to our heavenly Father and, consequently, should be to us also. The cause of disunity seems clear: it comes about because we fail to dispense to others the grace we ourselves have received from God. Our text for today urges us to 'keep the unity of the Spirit through the bond of peace'. There is an unbreakable unity in the Trinity which God desires to see reflected in His Church.

Think of this: there has never been an argument among the members of the Trinity, never a quarrel, never a disagreement. Sometimes we find it difficult to get on with one another for a few days; the Father, Son and Holy Spirit have existed for all eternity without a single dispute. Unity matters to each member of the Trinity, and matters to them more than we can ever realise. Then shouldn't unity matter to us? Notice that our text does not tell us to *build* unity; we are simply instructed to *keep* it. From God's point of view there is one flock and one Shepherd (see John 10:1-6). Unity is not something to be created but something to be protected.

**FURTHER STUDY**

Psa. 133:1-3;
Eph. 4:20-32

1. Where does God pour out blessing?

2. How could our words strengthen or destroy unity?

But how do we do that? How do we 'make every effort to keep the unity of the Spirit'? Do we abandon our convictions, compromise our beliefs, water down our doctrines? No, but when a dispute does arise we must make the effort to disagree agreeably. God has created us as choosing beings. We can choose to be either gracious or ungracious. The next time you feel you have to disagree with someone, remember you have a choice: you can disagree disagreeably or disagree agreeably. The choice is always yours.

**Father, I accept that I can disagree agreeably or disagree disagreeably. From now on I will choose to pass on the grace You have given to me, and when I have to disagree, I will do so agreeably. The grace is Yours, the choice is mine. Amen.**

# 'The fumes of ungrace'

### FOR READING & MEDITATION – MARK 9:33-50

'Have salt in yourselves, and be at peace with each other.' (v.50)

'**H**ow is it,' says one writer, 'that Christians called to dispense the aroma of grace instead emit the noxious fumes of ungrace?' How indeed? Permit this personal question: if you have a problem in dispensing 'the aroma of grace' in your relationships, are you willing to make every effort to discover why? Assuming your answer is 'Yes', let me see if I can help you.

One of the first things to consider is the need to accept people as they are. This has been described as 'the first law in good relationships'. Keep in mind that acceptance does not mean approval; it means accepting that the person is the way he or she is and that you respect them as persons even though you cannot approve of anything that is unbiblical.

**FURTHER STUDY**

John 4:1-9, 27-42; 2 Cor. 2:14-17

1. How did Jesus break cultural barriers of rejection?

2. How can we spread the fragrance of Christ?

From the passage we have read today we discover that the disciples had been arguing with each other about which of them was the greatest. Jesus responded by standing a child in their midst and saying, 'Whoever welcomes [or accepts] one of these little children in my name welcomes me …' (v.37). The point Jesus appeared to be making was this: acceptance is the first step to unity. Not agreement, not approval, not negotiation, not arbitration – acceptance. John was troubled by this answer and thought it too simplistic. Perhaps he said in effect, 'We saw someone casting out demons in Your name. Do we accept him? Surely we can't always go around accepting everyone.' It seems the Son of Thunder (see Mark 3:17) had a problem with acceptance. His view at that time was that fences have to be built, agreements negotiated, boundaries established. But not in this case. How accepting are little children. We must make the effort to be the same.

**Gracious heavenly Father, help me to be a more accepting person, but may I never let anyone think that my acceptance of them signifies approval of behaviour that is unbiblical. Give me the skill to do this in the way Your Son did. Amen.**

# A long way to go

**FOR READING & MEDITATION - ROMANS 15:1-13**

'Accept one another, then, just as Christ accepted you,
in order to bring praise to God.' (v.7)

**W**e spend another day considering 'the first law of relationships' – acceptance. This is something that with thought and consideration anyone can put into effect, but it is a skill made easier by grace. There are many other things we may need to know about dispensing grace, but it is outside the scope of these present meditations to go into them one by one. I am focusing only on acceptance because that is the first step to unity. Unless we learn this, all the other skills, such as negotiating, establishing boundaries, and so on, will not come together.

Paul, in chapter 14 of his letter to the Romans, had raised the matter of whether or not it was right to eat meat – obviously something the believers were struggling with. How does he advise them to deal with their disagreement? By having two churches – one for the meat eaters and one for vegetarians? No, he says, 'Accept one another, then, just as Christ accepted you.' In asking us, through Paul, to accept each other, God is not telling us to do something He has not done. If God can tolerate my mistakes then ought I not to tolerate yours? If God allows me, a man with a history of mistakes and failures, to call Him Father shouldn't I extend the same grace to you? Shame on me if I don't.

The Church, someone has commented, is like Noah's ark. If it weren't for the storm on the outside we wouldn't be able to stand the stench on the inside. We have a long way to go to demonstrate the degree of unity which the Father has with the Son – the unity for which Christ prayed in John 17. Do you think our Lord would pray a prayer that had no possibility of being answered? I don't think so either.

## FURTHER STUDY

Acts 10:9-29;
Gal. 2:11-16

1. What did God reveal to Peter?

2. Why did Peter still have a long way to go?

**Father, the more I consider this issue the more I realise how pained Your heart must be by the squabbles and disagreements You see amongst Your children. You have given us grace. Please help us to use it. In Jesus' name. Amen.**

# 'Brother- and sister-bashers'

### FOR READING & MEDITATION - COLOSSIANS 4:7-18

'Epaphras ... is always wrestling in prayer for you, that you may stand firm in all the will of God ...' (v.12)

**H**ow different the Church would appear in the eyes of the world if all Christians related to each other with grace. One preacher I know refers to Christians who can't get along with each other as 'brother- and sister-bashers'. And there are already too many of them roaming around on the spiritual scene. Nothing catches the attention of the world more than Christians coming to blows with each other. Paul, in Ephesians 6:10 (NKJV), talks about wrestling not with flesh and blood but with principalities and powers. How sad when we believers reverse that and spend our time wrestling not with principalities and powers but with flesh and blood.

**FURTHER STUDY**

1 John 3:11-20; 4:7-21

1. What is the proof that we love others?

2. What is the proof that we love God?

A while ago I read about something humorous that happened in connection with two evangelistic crusades that were held in an American city, one immediately after the other. The venue for both crusades was a small indoor stadium in the city. In between the crusades, and for one night only, a wrestling match had been booked. Those entering the stadium for the first crusade were amused to see the announcement in lights over the stadium entrance:

*Programme for the next two weeks:*
*Evangelist Jack Van Impe*
*Wrestling*
*Rex Humbard*

If the world is to be won for Jesus, we simply must take this matter of relating to one another in grace more seriously. We owe it to Christ, to each other, *and to the world* to do so.

**My Father and my God, help us become people who, like Epaphras, wrestle *for* our brothers and sisters rather than *with* them. Forgive us for bringing grace into disgrace. Amen.**

# Still feeling indebted

**FOR READING & MEDITATION - MATTHEW 18:21-35**

'The servant's master took pity on him, cancelled the debt
and let him go.' (v.27)

**Y**et another characteristic of those who walk free is this: *they know how to enter into the freedom that grace provides.* They understand that their Master has forgiven them an insurmountable debt and that He doesn't demand reimbursement. 'Ah,' I hear you say, 'I believe that but I wouldn't say I am "walking free".' Well, let's consider this matter carefully, for you may find that though you believe it in your head, it has not yet reached your heart. After years of listening to people sharing their struggles, I have come to the conclusion that by far the biggest single difficulty evangelical Christians struggle with is the failure to live a 'debt-free' existence. Let's explore this further.

The servant in the passage we have read today had a serious problem. Somehow he had run up a massive debt; the *Amplified Bible* tells us it was 'probably about $10,000,000'. Now it is important to realise that Jesus is deliberately using an exaggerated amount here to make it clear that the servant's debt was far greater than his ability to pay. That's the main point Jesus is making here. The king to whom he owed the debt decided to call it in and ordered the servant to take immediate steps for its repayment. Falling to his knees, the servant begs for time to pay, whereupon the king decides to cancel the debt and set him free.

The servant then goes out and comes across a man who owes him a mere pittance (about $20, says the *Amplified Bible*) and, because he is unable to repay the money, has him put in prison. Why did he act in this way? One explanation is this: he still *felt* in debt. The good news he had been given was still in his head and had never reached his heart.

**FURTHER STUDY**

Gen. 17:14;
Gal. 3:1-5; 5:1-12

1. What is the importance of circumcision?

2. What are we free from?

**Father, I realise that it is one thing to know my debt has been paid; it is another to let the impact of that reach my heart. Right now I open my heart to the wonder of being 'debt free'. Deepen my appreciation of this. In Jesus' name. Amen.**

# Thank you!

A huge thank you for all you do to support the
ministry of CWR. Your prayers and generous
financial giving have enabled us to meet the
spiritual needs of thousands of people, by
sending them our books and DVDs. Many men,
women and children, some yet to develop
a faith, new Christians and those who need
support in difficult times, have been touched
and changed. And the impact has been
worldwide – from India to the Middle East,
from Kazakhstan to China.

Here's just a snapshot of the difference you
have made in recent years:

**85,000 free resources released into prisons**,
helping men and women find hope in Jesus.

**29,000 Bible-reading materials sent to
children and pastors in Africa**, providing
inspiration and encouragement.

**9,000 Christian books placed in UK libraries**,
making the gospel more accessible.

**40,000 free books on biblical meditation
printed and distributed to individuals and
churches**, helping them to go deeper in their
Bible study.

**200,000 resources provided to those taking the first steps in the Christian faith.**

And in recent months you have helped us to send **5,000 special books to service personnel and their families**, offering them love and support.

Each publication represents a fresh start, a relationship restored, a deeper walk with God. So we thank you for your selfless generosity, which helps to change lives.

Each one of these seeds sown God grows and multiplies, as those who have been changed reach out to their families, churches and communities.

Thank you!

# Forgiven

FOR READING & MEDITATION – ROMANS 6:15-23

'For the wages of sin is death, but the gift of God is eternal life in Christ Jesus our Lord.' (v.23)

Today we continue reflecting on the story told in Matthew 18:21-35 of the servant who, having been forgiven a massive debt, goes out and demands that a man who owes him a paltry sum be cast into prison. Something is wrong with this picture. It doesn't make sense that a man forgiven such a large sum would behave in this way towards someone who owed him such an insignificant amount. The account says: 'He grabbed him and began to choke him. "Pay back what you owe me!" he demanded' (Matt. 18:28). Are these the words of a man who has been set free? How could this happen? How could a man who was forgiven not forgive?

**FURTHER STUDY**

Gal. 4:8-11;
Heb. 10:1-18

1. What was Paul's concern?

2. How do we know no debt is outstanding?

We touched on one conclusion yesterday: he did not feel forgiven. The servant left the king's presence a free man, but he had not allowed the impact of such amazing grace to penetrate his heart. His problem was *unrealised forgiveness*. Many Christians are in this same state. They have been forgiven a massive debt – far beyond their power to repay – but the realisation of just how much they have been forgiven has never quite hit them. Their debt to God has been discharged through the payment made by Jesus on Calvary's cross, but they seem unable to enter into the freedom such a release should bring.

Are you in this place, I wonder? Has the realisation of how much you have been forgiven reached deep into your heart? Then take some time today to ponder just what it means to be forgiven. Earlier we touched on the holiness of God, and the fact that sin has consequences. But praise Him that because of His love for us He has paid the price for our sin in the death of His only Son, and we are completely forgiven and free to live for Him. What grace!

**Father, I think I am seeing more clearly that the *realisation* of sins forgiven is crucial in living effectively for You. I realise it to some degree. Please help me to realise it even more. In Jesus' name. Amen.**

# From minimum to maximum

**FOR READING & MEDITATION - LUKE 7:36-50**

'... her many sins have been forgiven - for she loved much.
But he who has been forgiven little loves little.' (v.47)

**A**s the issue we discussed yesterday is so important – the issue of unrealised forgiveness – we will spend another day reflecting on it. In today's text Jesus puts His finger on the matter we are discussing. Eugene Peterson, in *The Message*, expresses Jesus' words in this way: 'If the forgiveness is minimal, the gratitude is minimal.' Those who walk free, I have discovered, don't have a problem with unrealised forgiveness. They have a clear awareness that they have been forgiven a massive debt, a debt it would have been absolutely impossible for them to repay even if they had been given all eternity to repay it. And they are grateful for that forgiveness, more grateful than words can ever convey.

Focusing on the extent to which we have been forgiven is vital to the rest of our Christian life. Awareness of forgiveness brings not only feelings of freedom and gratitude to God but also a willingness to forgive those who have sinned against us. You see, only the truly forgiven can be forgiving. The truth is this: our pockets are empty while our debt runs into millions. We don't need a better salary in order to pay off the debt over a lifetime, we need a gift. Max Lucado says: 'We don't need swimming lessons, we need a lifesaver.'

Perhaps yesterday it was not possible for you to follow the suggestion I made to find a quiet place and ponder just how much you have been forgiven. If that was the case, try to do so today. Realise the enormity of the debt you owed to God and the grace He showed you in cancelling it. Think about that until your heart awakens fully to the news that the massive debt you owed to God has been forgiven. Forgiven!

**FURTHER STUDY**

Gal. 4:21-31;
1 Tim. 1:12-17

1. How does Paul contrast law and grace?

2. Of what was Paul constantly aware?

**O Father, I long to realise more and more the extent to which I have been forgiven, for I see that is the key to so many things in my spiritual life. Touch my heart, my mind, my imagination, as I reflect on this today. In Jesus' name. Amen.**

# 'Remember the duck'

**FOR READING & MEDITATION - ISAIAH 50:1-11**

'He who vindicates me is near. Who then will bring charges against me?' (v.8)

**O**ne of the consequences of unrealised forgiveness and of not entering into the freedom which forgiveness is meant to bring is that we become extremely vulnerable to the devil's untruths. Countless times I have counselled Christians who, though they have been forgiven, are still troubled by feelings of guilt. And nothing pleases the father of lies more than to find Christians in that condition, for he knows that his accusations will find their mark.

Once I read about a young boy and his sister who spent their summer holiday on their grandmother's farm. One day, while the boy was throwing stones, he accidentally hit his grandmother's pet duck and killed it. Rather than owning up, he took the duck and hid it in thick undergrowth. His sister, however, had witnessed the incident, and for a few days afterwards, whenever she wanted to persuade her brother to do something, she would whisper, 'Remember the duck.' Eventually the boy grew tired of being manipulated and confessed to his grandmother what he had done. To his surprise she said, 'I was standing at the window and saw what you did myself. Because I love you I decided to forgive you. But I did wonder how long you would let your sister make a slave out of you.'

**FURTHER STUDY**

John 8:31-36;
Rom. 6:15-22

1. How can we be slaves to sin?

2. How can we be truly set free?

So many Christians are in a similar position; they have been pardoned but they are slaves to the accuser (the name given to Satan in Revelation 12:10). Satan has no higher goal than to take you to court and press charges. He paces backwards and forwards calling your name, listing your faults, naming your sins. Let's be clear: because Jesus shed His blood for you on Calvary, the Judge has released you. You are free. You need no longer fear the court.

**Father, I know the power of grace is stronger than any power Satan may wield against me. But head knowledge is not enough. The realisation must possess me, even obsess me. Grant that it may be so. In Jesus' name. Amen.**

# The first principle

MON
18 FEB

**FOR READING & MEDITATION - LUKE 6:37-42**

'Forgive, and you will be forgiven.' (v.37)

**N**othing, we have been saying, is more vital if we are to live effectively as Christians than entering into the freedom that grace provides. It is one thing to be pronounced free but it is another thing to feel free. The issue of unrealised forgiveness, I believe, is the chief cause of a failure to forgive others. If we really understood how much we have been forgiven then we would have little difficulty in forgiving others. Sins others have committed against you (though they may be painful and cruel) cannot compare with the massive debt you built up by your denial of God's right to rule in your heart.

I realise that those of you reading these lines who have been the victim of abuse or brutality may find that difficult to accept. I would not judge you or condemn you if you said, 'I can never forgive that person for what he (or she) did to me.' But what I would say to you is this, the more you reflect on the wonder of how much you have been forgiven, so it will become easier to forgive even the worst that has been committed against you.

There are many principles to consider in relation to forgiveness, but this without any doubt is the first principle: the more we realise how much we have been forgiven the more forgiving we will be. I was interested to read this in David Seamand's book *Healing Grace*: 'I am convinced that the basic cause of some of the most disturbing emotional and spiritual problems which trouble evangelical Christians is the failure to receive and live out God's unconditional grace and the corresponding failure to offer that grace to others. I encounter this problem in the counselling room more than any other hang-up.' And so, I must add, have I.*

### FURTHER STUDY

Gen. 50:15-21;
Col. 3:12-14

1. Contrast Joseph and his brothers' attitudes to forgiveness.

2. Why should we forgive?

**Heavenly Father, may I be so rich in the feelings that come from the knowledge of forgiveness that I dispense forgiveness prodigally to others. You forgave me not grudgingly but graciously. May I act in a similar manner. Amen.**

*For more on this issue, see Ron Kallmier and Sheila Jacobs' book *Insight into Forgiveness*, published by CWR.

# The performance trap

**FOR READING & MEDITATION – ROMANS 11:1-12**

'So too, at the present time there is a remnant chosen by grace.'
(v.5)

**W**e look now at one last characteristic of those whose walk with God is free and unhindered: *they are people who know how to avoid the performance trap.* You may not have come across the expression 'the performance trap' before, so let me explain it now.

The performance trap is living out our lives with the idea that we must always *do something* in order to be accepted by God. Philip Yancey says this, 'Grace sounds a startling note of contradiction ... and every day I must pray anew for the ability to hear its message.' If you are anything like me, you will need to remind yourself every day that we are precious to God not because of what we do but because of who we are. That does not mean our service for God is unimportant or that God does not enjoy it. However, the ground of our acceptance is not what we do for Him but what He does for us.

**FURTHER STUDY**

Deut. 7:6-9;
Eph. 1:1-14

1. Why did God choose Israel?

2. Why did God choose us?

In the fourth and fifth centuries there were two notable Bible teachers. One was named Augustine and the other Pelagius. Augustine believed that salvation was a matter of grace, and that had God not taken the initiative in saving us then we would not be saved. Pelagius took the opposite view and believed that people can take the initial steps towards salvation using their own effort and do not require grace to do so. Augustine, I believe, held the right view. Pelagius methodically worked to please God, Augustine rejoiced in the fact that, as the verse before us today puts it, he was 'chosen by grace'.

Eugene Peterson claims that many Christians are Augustinian in theory but Pelagian in practice. In other words, they work to please God rather than rejoicing in the fact that because they are in Christ He is already pleased with them.

**Father, can it be that I am Augustinian in theory but Pelagian in practice? Help me examine my heart to see if this is so. And if it is then release me from dependence on works to dependence on grace. In Jesus' name. Amen.**

# Obsessed by grace

**FOR READING & MEDITATION – 2 TIMOTHY 1:1-18**

'... who has saved us and called us to a holy life – not because of
anything we have done ...' (v.9)

In all of us there is this strange sense that we must *do
something* in order to be accepted. It comes, of course,
from our old human nature that is shot through with a
desire to earn approval rather than accept it as a matter
of grace. Daniel Rowlands, a Welsh revivalist, wrote, 'No
sooner do we become Christians and accept salvation by
grace than there is an impulse in us to earn God's approval,
and we set about obsessively trying to please Him by our
good works.' Multitudes of Christians do this, and when
they do they fall into the performance trap.

Everywhere you look in Paul's writing, as we
said earlier, he has something to say about grace.
The word 'grace' appears in the first few verses of
every one of his letters, and he signs off every letter
with the word 'grace'. Grace was the central motif
of his life. Transformed on the Damascus Road,
he never got over the fact that grace sought him,
grace bought him, and grace taught him. Frederick
Buechner, an American Bible commentator, says
of Paul's greetings to his readers, 'Grace is the best
he [Paul] can wish them because grace is the best
he himself ever received.'

Paul emphasised grace to such a degree because
he knew what would happen to Christians if they responded
to the instinct to try and earn God's love. They would
become workaholics, driven by the idea that God would
stop loving them if they were not being busy. Paul counted
himself as the worst of sinners (1 Tim. 1:15), and he knew
beyond doubt that God loves people because of who He is,
not because of what they do. We simply must get this truth
into our heads, for if we don't then we will end up working
to be saved instead of working *because* we are saved.

**FURTHER
STUDY**

Rom. 3:19-31;
Eph. 2:1-10

1. Why can we
not boast in
our salvation?

2. Contrast
the law of
works and the
law of faith.

**Heavenly Father, if there is an impulse in me to try to earn Your
approval, and I am caught in trying to please You by my good
works, then deliver me from it right now I pray. May I live by
grace, not by graft. Amen.**

# 'I am the one Jesus loves'

## FOR READING & MEDITATION - JOHN 20:1-18

'So she came running to Simon Peter and the other disciple, the one Jesus loved ...' (v.2)

**A**ll commentators agree that when John wrote the phrase found in our text for today – 'the one Jesus loved' – he was referring to himself. Brennan Manning, author of *The Ragamuffin Gospel*, a book I have come to treasure, said in one of his seminars, 'If John were to be asked, "What is your primary identity in life?" he would not reply, "I am a disciple, an apostle, an evangelist, an author of one of the four Gospels," but rather, "I am the one Jesus loves."' What would it mean for us, I wonder, if we saw ourselves first and foremost not in the roles we play in life – as ministers, car mechanics, nurses, schoolteachers, engineers, shop assistants, and so on – but as 'the one Jesus loves'? I will tell you what it would mean: we would cease trying to impress the Lord by our performance and rejoice in the fact that we are the objects of His affection.

**FURTHER STUDY**

Rom. 4:1-16;
Gal. 2:17-21

1. How is Abraham an example of salvation by grace?

2. What could Paul say of Jesus' feelings towards him?

The story is told of an Irish priest who, while walking through his parish one day, saw an elderly peasant kneeling by the side of the road praying. The priest was struck by the sight, and quietly going up to the man he remarked, 'You must be very close to God.' The peasant looked up from his prayers, thought for a moment, and said, 'Yes, He's very fond of me.' That peasant was probably closer to God than most because he saw himself as the one who was loved.

We must get it in our hearts that there is nothing we can do to make God love us more. No amount of spiritual discipline, attendance of seminars, study of the Bible, can make God love us more than He already does. He loves us as much as it is possible for an infinite God to love. That's where our true identity must be found – in being loved.

**O Father, how I need this word. Help me to see even more clearly that my identity must be in who I am not in what I do. And who am I? I am the one whom Jesus loves. Thank You, dear Father. Amen.**

# NEXT ISSUE

## Eat, Pray, Share

What do you call it in your church? 'The Sacrament', 'The Lord's Supper', 'The Lord's Table', 'The Eucharist', 'The Breaking of Bread'?

Join us next issue, as we meditate on the Easter story, with a special focus on the service of Holy Communion. Recall or discover for the first time the deep significance of gathering as Christians to commemorate Jesus' sacrifice for us. In particular, we will explore:

**Every Day with Jesus**

MAR/APR 2013

## Eat, Pray, Share

'While they were eating, Jesus took bread, gave thanks and broke it ... saying, "Take and eat; this is my body."'
Matthew 26:26

Be revived and refreshed by God's Word   **CWR**

- What we are remembering
- The call to humility
- The importance of being together
- A continuous festival.

Let's allow the wonder of God's love to lead us to renewed thankfulness and commitment.

Also available as ebook/esubscription

OBTAIN YOUR COPY FROM
**CWR, a Christian bookshop or National Distributor.**
If you would like to take out a subscription, see the order form at the back of these notes.

# 'The tyranny of the oughts'

## FOR READING & MEDITATION - GALATIANS 5:1-6

'You who are trying to be justified by law have been alienated from Christ; you have fallen away from grace.' (v.4)

Today we ask ourselves what are some of the signs that Christians are caught up in the performance trap? The six most common signs are these: First, a never-ending battle with what has been described as the 'tyranny of the oughts' – the feeling that one *ought* always to be trying hard to please God and, however hard the effort, that one *ought* always to try harder. Second, an overwhelming sense of guilt and condemnation even when there is no known sin of which to repent. Third, a high degree of anxiety. Fourth, a sense of low esteem from constantly belittling oneself. Fifth, repression of the emotions, and sixth, a spirit of legalism resulting from an oversensitive conscience.

**FURTHER STUDY**

Luke 18:9-14;
Gal. 6:12-16

1. Contrast the Pharisee and the tax collector.

2. What is the only thing that counts?

Do you identify with some of these signs? Perhaps you feel like the missionary who once told me, 'I never feel that God is pleased with me unless I am working myself to death, I am weighed down with some sickness, or I am at the point of exhaustion.' This lady was trapped on the treadmill of performance and saw no way of getting off. At the heart of the performance trap is a diabolical lie that our spiritual life depends entirely on how we perform. There were people in the Galatian church with that outlook, as Paul tells us so clearly in the passage we have read today. They started out living by grace but fell into the performance trap. What is common to all who fall into the performance trap is the belief that God is not pleased with their efforts.

If I am describing you then settle the issue once and for all: God does not delight in you for what you do but for who you are, a child of His grace. If you never did another hour of service for Him He would not love you less.

**O Father, grant that I may never fall away from grace in the sense that I begin to depend more on my resources than on Yours. Dependence on works means I am alienated from You. Grant that may never be so. In Jesus' name. Amen.**

# Who holds who?

**FOR READING & MEDITATION - JUDE 17-25**

'To him who is able to keep you from falling and to present you
before his glorious presence ...' (v.24)

**Y**esterday we concluded with the statement, 'If you never
did another hour of service for Him He would not love
you less.' At first that statement might seem dangerous,
as it might encourage some to give less to God in terms of
their time, talents and treasure. Not so, however.

Some years ago I talked to a woman who was caught up
in the performance trap (doing dutiful things because she
believed her acceptance by God depended on this). I said to
her, 'I know what I am going to say is not really possible,
but suppose you could lie down on this floor and go to sleep
for a whole year. When you awoke do you believe

**FURTHER STUDY**

Ezek. 36:22-36;
John 10:27-30

1. What did
Israel do to gain
God's favour?

2. Who
holds us?

God would love you as much as He did when you
fell asleep?' She thought for a moment and replied,
'I don't believe so.' 'Why?' I asked. 'Well,' she said,
'I would not have read my Bible, attended prayer
meetings, given my tithes, not done anything to
bring people to Christ ...' 'No, I don't think that
would make any difference,' I said quietly. 'This
is where you perhaps misunderstand. God would
love you when you awoke as much as He did when
you fell asleep. Nothing in you can extinguish
His love, and nothing in you can increase it.' That simple
statement seemed to break through her barrier of legalism
and she caught such a glimpse of God's unconditional love
that in a matter of days she became a transformed person.

A car hire company used to have as its slogan 'We try
harder'. The Christian life is not a matter of trying but
trusting – trusting that the grace by which we're saved
is powerful enough to sustain us also. It is not a case of
needing to hold on to God but of letting Him hold us. Never
forget that.

**O Father, I must grasp this for I see it can mean all the difference
between success and failure in my Christian life. It's not
necessary for me to hold on to You because You are holding on to
me. Thank You, my Father. Amen.**

# 'An altogether Christian'

### FOR READING & MEDITATION - GALATIANS 4:1-7

'So you are no longer a slave, but a son; and since you are a son,
God has made you also an heir.' (v.7)

**O**n 24 May 1738 at a quarter to nine in the evening, John Wesley, an Anglican clergyman and missionary, sat in a house in Aldersgate in the city of London listening to someone reading from Luther's Preface to the Epistle to Romans. As he heard Luther's description of the change which God works in the heart through faith in Christ, he said that he felt his 'heart strangely warmed'. He added, 'I felt I did trust in Christ, Christ alone, for salvation; and an assurance was given me that He had taken away my sins, even mine, and saved me from the law of sin and death.'

**FURTHER STUDY**

Luke 15:11-24;
John 15:9-17

1. What surprised the wayward son?

2. How did Jesus change the relationship with His disciples?

John Wesley became what he called 'an altogether Christian', and said also that whereas before he had the religion of a servant, after his conversion he had that of a son.

It is true, of course, that we are called God's servants in Scripture, and that cannot be denied, but when it comes to describing the relationship as opposed to the role, the best word to use is 'son' or 'child'. A servant is appreciated on the basis of what he (or she) does; a child on the basis of who he is. The servant starts out determined to please the master; the child knows he already has his parents' pleasure. The servant is accepted because of his workmanship; the child because of a relationship.

When a servant fails, as Dr David Seamands points out, 'his or her whole position is at stake. In a normal home when a child fails or violates the laws of the home he or she may feel grieved that they have blundered or been ineffectual, and will submit themselves to discipline, but they know in their hearts they still belong and are deeply loved.'

Always remember, your role may be that of a servant but your relationship is that of a child.

**Father, thank You for reminding me that though my role might be that of a servant, my relationship is that of Your child. Your Son taught us to call You 'Father', not 'Master'. You are my Master, but first of all my Father. I am so glad. Amen.**

**FOR READING & MEDITATION – ROMANS 5:12-21**

'But where sin increased, grace increased all the more ...' (v.20)

'**M**ost Christians,' says Charles Swindoll, 'have been better trained to expect and handle their sin than to expect and enjoy their freedom.' The church in which I was brought up was inclined to be legalistic (it was still a wonderful church, for all that). However, I found that once I began to appreciate that we are not only saved by grace but also sustained by it, I gained far more victory over life's difficulties than I did in my legalistic days. I shall never forget the moment when the Holy Spirit illuminated the words of today's text to my heart. Though I had read them many times before, on this particular occasion they exploded in my heart. It was as if God said to me, 'You were once enslaved to all kinds of passions but now you are free from that slavery. Where sin abounds, grace superabounds.'

Many Christians begin the day with a fear that they may falter, and end it with a list of things they feel they have to confess. And if one evening the list is not very long, they fear they may have overlooked 'hidden sins'. 'Perhaps I have become proud,' they say to themselves. Are freed people supposed to live such a fearful existence? The question we must ask ourselves is this: are we emancipated or not? If we are free then let's live as if we are. 'So if the Son sets you free,' says Jesus, 'you will be free indeed' (John 8:36).

How much better it is to begin every day with thoughts of love rather than defeat, to awake to grace not shame, to face every situation in the confidence that we can fail without losing our relationship with our heavenly Father. I assure you that if you walk in the knowledge of that, it will enable you to fail less.

**FURTHER STUDY**

Rom. 8:1-17;
Gal. 5:22-25

1. What picture does Paul present of the Spirit-filled person?

2. What is the result of walking in the Spirit?

**Gracious Father, may I begin every day with the thought that it is possible not to sin. Help me to adopt a more positive approach to life, knowing that grace is strong enough to overcome every temptation. For Jesus' sake. Amen.**

# Grace comes with everything

**FOR READING & MEDITATION - PROVERBS 3:27-35**

'He mocks proud mockers but gives grace to the humble.' (v.34)

**O**ne thing we need to do above all others to get out of the performance trap is to humbly confess that we have fallen into it. So right now let your mind run over the past few months and years. Have you fallen into the trap of thinking that you must always *do something* to be accepted by God? Then I have to tell you that underlying that thought is pride. Does that surprise you? You see, pride works not only in downright hostility to God but it is there also when we relegate Him to irrelevance.

If you have come to the point where you are depending more on your own resources to run your life than on the grace God gives, it is time for an act of repentance. Read again the words of today's text: '[The Lord] mocks proud mockers but gives grace to the humble.' Grace is available for every aspect of the Christian life, and if you have been caught in the performance trap then there is grace flowing towards you now to enable you to repent. And more, much more than you need.

**FURTHER STUDY**

Isa. 57:14-19;
James 4:6-10

1. What is the contradiction in God's addresses?

2. What is promised to the humble?

Once I was in Memphis, Tennessee, and went with a friend into a diner for breakfast. I ordered bacon and eggs – just bacon and eggs. However, when my order arrived it came with something called 'grits' – a kind of porridge popular in the deep South. 'I don't think I ordered grits,' I exclaimed. The waitress replied, 'Maybe you didn't, but at breakfast time grits come with everything.' It's the same with grace. It comes with everything in the Christian life. It is there right now to help you ask God to forgive you for misunderstanding the gospel of free grace and come to the glorious realisation that you don't have to do anything to earn His love. You already have it. Pray this prayer with me:

**O God, I confess my instinct is to do something to earn Your love. Forgive me for harbouring it. I turn from all thoughts of trying to earn Your approval to rejoicing in the fact I already have it. Thank You, my Father. Amen.**

# The gift we needed most

**FOR READING & MEDITATION – 2 CORINTHIANS 9:6-15**

'Thanks be to God for his indescribable gift!' (v.15)

**W**e are coming now to the end of our meditations on the theme of grace. I feel somewhat like the writer to the Hebrews, who said, 'And what more shall I say? I do not have time to tell about Gideon, Barak, Samson, Jephthah, David, Samuel and the prophets ...' (Heb. 11:32). Clearly he had run out of time but not out of things to say. It is the same with grace. Much has been said in the last eight weeks but I assure you more, much more, *could* be said.

A friend once sent me a Christmas card with these words from Charles Sell's book *Unfinished Business*. They impressed me deeply and form a fitting conclusion to what we have been meditating on over these past weeks:

**FURTHER STUDY**

Luke 1:67-79; 2:8-20

1. How have we been enabled by God's mercy through Christ?

2. What was the angel's message?

*If our greatest need had been information,*
*God would have sent us an educator.*
*If our greatest need had been technology,*
*God would have sent us a scientist.*
*If our greatest need had been money,*
*God would have sent us an economist.*
*If our greatest need had been pleasure,*
*God would have sent us an entertainer.*
*But our greatest need was forgiveness,*
*so God sent us a Saviour!*

When, on that first Christmas morning, Mary looked at the face of her newborn son, I wonder, did she realise that she was unwrapping for humanity what Paul calls God's 'indescribable gift'? That indescribable gift of grace was the gift we needed most.

**O great redeeming God, how can I ever sufficiently thank You for so graciously sending Your Son to seek and save the lost? Since I have found Him, or more correctly He has found me, life has been so different. Thank You, Father. Amen.**

# It really is amazing

**FOR READING & MEDITATION – REVELATION 22:12-21**

'The grace of the Lord Jesus be with God's people. Amen.' (v.21)

**D**oesn't it strike you as fascinating that the last word in the Bible is a word about grace? And so it should be, for it is not only the first word in everything but the last word also. Nothing is greater than grace. Nothing! When John Newton wrote his hymn about grace he used the word 'amazing' to describe it. As someone who constantly uses words I have tried to think of a better word to describe it, but there just isn't one. It really is *amazing*.

Maybe you have seen the documentary made by Bill Moyers on the hymn 'Amazing Grace'. One of the scenes

**FURTHER STUDY**

2 Pet. 3:17-18;
Rev. 5:1-14

1. What should we seek?

2. How can weeping turn to rejoicing and worship?

shows Wembley Stadium in London, where several bands had gathered for a rock festival. The concert lasted for 12 hours, and you can imagine the mood of the crowd by the end of that time, many of them high on drink and drugs. The festival concluded with a song from an opera singer by the name of Jessye Norman – a beautiful African American woman. She chose as her song 'Amazing Grace'. Without any accompaniment she began to sing slowly:

*Amazing grace! how sweet the sound,*
*That saved a wretch like me!*
*I once was lost, but now am found;*
*Was blind, but now I see.*

By the time she reached the last verse a strange power had descended on the stadium. All was quiet.

Non-Christians as well as Christians are amazed by grace. Though we may not realise it all the time, that is what we all thirst for. And when it is seen – not just sung – then all the world will fall silent before it. It's amazing. Utterly amazing.

**O God, I bow my heart in deepest gratitude that grace has wooed me and won me. May I take down every barrier that more may come in. Help me open myself to all You have to give me, today and ever more. In Jesus' name. Amen.**

# ORDER FORM

## 4 EASY WAYS TO ORDER:

1. Phone in your credit card order: **01252 784710** (Mon-Fri, 9.30am - 5pm)
2. Visit our Online Store at **www.cwr.org.uk/store**
3. Send this form together with your payment to:
   **CWR, Waverley Abbey House, Waverley Lane, Farnham, Surrey GU9 8EP**
4. Visit your local Christian bookshop

r a list of our National Distributors, who supply countries outside the UK, visit www.cwr.org.uk/distributors

### YOUR DETAILS (REQUIRED FOR ORDERS AND DONATIONS)

Name: _____  CWR ID No. (if known): _____

Home Address: _____

Postcode: _____

Telephone No. (for queries): _____  Email: _____

### PUBLICATIONS

| TITLE | QTY | PRICE | TOTAL |
|-------|-----|-------|-------|
|  |  |  |  |
|  |  |  |  |
|  |  |  |  |
|  |  |  |  |
|  |  | **Total publications** |  |

All CWR adult Bible-reading notes are also available in ebook and email subscription format.
Visit www.cwr.org.uk for further information.

**UK p&p:** up to £24.99 = **£2.99**; £25.00 and over = **FREE**

**Elsewhere p&p:** up to £10 = **£4.95**; £10.01 - £50 = **£6.95**; £50.01 - £99.99 = **£10**; £100 and over = **£30**

Please allow 14 days for delivery    **Total publications and p&p A** [ ]

### SUBSCRIPTIONS* (NON DIRECT DEBIT)

| | QTY | PRICE (INCLUDING P&P) | | | TOTAL |
|---|-----|------|--------|-----------|-------|
| | | UK | Europe | Elsewhere | |
| Every Day with Jesus (1yr, 6 issues) | | £15.95 | £19.95 | Please contact nearest National Distributor or CWR direct | |
| Large Print Every Day with Jesus (1yr, 6 issues) | | £15.95 | £19.95 | | |
| Inspiring Women Every Day (1yr, 6 issues) | | £15.95 | £19.95 | | |
| Life Every Day (Jeff Lucas) (1yr, 6 issues) | | £15.95 | £19.95 | | |
| Cover to Cover Every Day (1yr, 6 issues) | | £15.95 | £19.95 | | |
| Mettle: 14-18s (1yr, 3 issues) | | £14.50 | £16.60 | | |
| YP's: 11-15s (1yr, 6 issues) | | £15.95 | £19.95 | | |
| Topz: 7-11s (1yr, 6 issues) | | £15.95 | £19.95 | | |
| **Total Subscriptions** (Subscription prices already include postage and packing) | | | | **B** | |

ase circle which bimonthly issue you would like your subscription to commence from:
/Feb  Mar/Apr  May/Jun  Jul/Aug  Sep/Oct  Nov/Dec

nly use this section for subscriptions paid for by credit/debit card or
heque. For Direct Debit subscriptions see overleaf.

**CONTINUED OVERLEAF >>**

**‹‹ SEE PREVIOUS PAGE FOR START OF ORDER FORM**

## PAYMENT DETAILS

☐ I enclose a cheque/PO made payable to CWR for the amount of: £ _____

☐ Please charge my credit/debit card.

**Cardholder's name** (in BLOCK CAPITALS) _____

Card No. ☐☐☐☐ ☐☐☐☐ ☐☐☐☐ ☐☐☐☐

Expires end ☐☐☐☐

Security Code ☐☐☐

---

**GIFT TO CWR** ☐ Please send me an acknowledgement of my gift      **C** _____

---

## GIFT AID (YOUR HOME ADDRESS REQUIRED, SEE OVERLEAF)

*giftaid it*

I am a UK taxpayer and want CWR to reclaim the tax on all my donations for the four years prior to this year **and on** all donations I make from the date of this Gift Aid declaration until further notice.*

**Taxpayer's Full Name** (in BLOCK CAPITALS) _____

**Signature** _____   **Date** _____

*I understand I must pay an amount of Income/Capital Gains Tax at least equal to the tax the charity reclaims in the tax year.

**GRAND TOTAL** (Total of A, B, & C) ☐

---

## SUBSCRIPTIONS BY DIRECT DEBIT (UK BANK ACCOUNT HOLDERS ONLY)

Subscriptions cost £15.95 (except *Mettle*: £14.50) for one year for delivery within the UK. Please tick relevant boxes and fill in the form

☐ *Every Day with Jesus* (1yr, 6 issues)
☐ Large Print *Every Day with Jesus* (1yr, 6 issues)
☐ *Inspiring Women Every Day* (1yr, 6 issues)
☐ *Life Every Day* (Jeff Lucas) (1yr, 6 issues)

☐ *Cover to Cover Every Day* (1yr, 6 issues)
☐ *Mettle*: 14-18s (1yr, 3 issues)
☐ *YP's*: 11-15s (1yr, 6 issues)
☐ *Topz*: 7-11s (1yr, 6 issues)

**Issue to commence**
☐ Jan/Feb ☐ Jul/Aug
☐ Mar/Apr ☐ Sep/Oct
☐ May/Jun ☐ Nov/De

---

**CWR**

Instruction to your Bank or Building Society to pay by Direct Debit

**DIREC Debi**

Please fill in the form and send to: CWR, Waverley Abbey House, Waverley Lane, Farnham, Surrey GU9 8EP

**Name and full postal address of your Bank or Building Society**

To: The Manager _____ Bank/Building Society

Address _____

Postcode _____

**Name(s) of Account Holder(s)** _____

**Branch Sort Code** ☐☐ ☐☐ ☐☐

**Bank/Building Society account number** ☐☐☐☐☐☐☐☐

**Originator's Identification Number**

| 4 | 2 | 0 | 4 | 8 | 7 |
|---|---|---|---|---|---|

**Reference**

**Instruction to your Bank or Building Society**

Please pay CWR Direct Debits from the account detailed in this Instruction to the safeguards assured by the Direct Debit Guarantee.

I understand that this instruction may remain with CWR and, if so, details wil passed electronically to my Bank/Building Society.

Signature(s) _____

Date _____

Banks and Building Societies may not accept Direct Debit Instructions for some types of account